By Their Valour

E. Doyle & J. McQuaid

Copyright © 2017 Emmet Doyle and Joanne McQuaid

All rights reserved.

ISBN: 1533606897

ISBN-13: 978 -1533606891

DEDICATIONS

Emmet Doyle

I would like to dedicate this work to three strong women within my own family. My grandmother, Elizabeth 'Hester' Doyle, who passed away in October 2010, my late cousin Sr. Clare Crockett, who was tragically killed in the Ecuadorian earthquake of April 2016, and my Godmother, Margaret, for all her support and guidance.

Joanne McQuaid

I'd like to thank my family for giving me the time to write this book. I'd especially like to thank my husband Mark and my son Daniel whose love and support have been my anchor through good times and bad.
Last but most certainly not least I'd like to send gratitude to my co-author and friend, Emmet Doyle. At times I know we both questioned what we had gotten ourselves into, but I know without his determination this book would never have been produced.

CONTENTS

Acknowledgments	7
1 Preface	9
2 Organised Warriors: Labour	13
3 Revolutionary Women	19
4 Women as defenders of the Northern State	52
5 Case Studies	65
6 Peacemakers	69
7 Appendices	90
8 Bibliography	97

ACKNOWLEDGMENTS

We would like to acknowledge the Deputy Keeper of the Records at the Public Record Office of Northern Ireland for use of historical files, and to all of those people who took time to talk to us and gave us support over the period it took us to complete this work.

1 PREFACE

Being from the City of Derry, a place where the role of women is venerated for the many years their labours kept the City alive, we were only too aware of how easy it can be for men throughout the history of this part of the world to dominate at the expense of great women.

Ireland has always been rested on a bedrock of patriarchy, dominated by the economic, social and cultural dominance of the male – either at home, at prayers or at the ballot box.

A focus on the male achievements, whatever their motivation and outcome, has long been a focus for writers and readers alike – stories about Collins, De Valera, Craig, Carson, Redmond, Adams, Spence – the list goes on and on.

What we risk losing in that focus is the indeterminable impact women have had on our society, and in forming the country we now live in. Women who forged states, who defended rights, who fought, created and who destroyed.

Furthermore, pigeonholing women by background, by motivation and by success or failure further impedes the understanding and appreciation of women and their own brand of valour. We seek in this work to shed light on some of the extraordinary women and their exploits through Ireland's recent history, not simply by Nationalist or Unionists, but by women of all colours and creeds.

We uncovered a number of disturbing pieces of information whilst completing this work, primarily and surprisingly, on those women who sought to defend the Northern state from terrorism by serving in the Armed Forces.

BY THEIR VALOUR

Local women who wanted to serve in the Ulster Defence Regiment, for example, were required to submit written permission from their husbands declaring that their service would not disturb their 'domestic responsibilities' at home – during a time when Republican women were serving long jail terms for seeking to overthrow the state, and even having children in our jails. Women were only permitted to serve widely in the infantry of the British Army in recent years.

This is made all the more surprising when we look at the Royal Ulster Constabulary and its successor. Women were not routinely armed despite the threat to their lives being equal to men on the front line of policing during the conflict.

Despite our efforts to determine otherwise, and using visual sources, without much assistance from the authorities, we feel comfortable to make another disturbing claim – service women who served the state have been omitted from some local official memorials to those who died during the conflict. It is of course possible that some non-resident female soldiers who lost their lives here are commemorated by their respective regiments at home, but on official regiments and memorial gardens here, from the information we have, they are omitted.

It may surprise some that we used the word 'valour' in this publication. However, we both agreed that we are not in a position to glean from the actions or thoughts of the women referred to in this work as to what constitutes bravery. It was brave to become a soldier, whomever you served – it was brave to step outside your front door and continue to provide a normal life for your family during times of peril and turmoil.

We have no interest here in, as we referred to, pigeonholing women – either IRA or UDA women as evil, or the state forces as virtuous – that is not for us to determine, we wish only that the role of their gender in shaping our lives be documented.

As part of the research for the book, we made trips on more than one occasion to Dublin and Belfast to access public records – in some instances this was particularly helpful, as was the case with Bridie – who you will read about. It is clear that on many occasions, the civil servants, soldiers and prison warders, the vast majority of whom were male, felt that women in relation to those involved in paramilitary activity did so unbeknownst to themselves – that they had in some way been forced into it, as no women could possibly want to be involved in such activity. Is that what made the contribution of women in that scenario so powerful?

PREFACE

It is evident that only from the early nineties did any meaningful social experiment take place locally to discover the views of women, their reasons for what they did or did not do, and its impact on our society. That work undertaken by scholars was largely sacrificed for political progress, as part of our work will demonstrate.

Women then had to build a new platform to take peace forward.

We hope this book can act as part of a testimony to the role they have played and will continue to play.

2 ORGANISED WARRIORS: WOMEN IN THE LABOUR MOVEMENT

Women throughout Ireland have played a significant role in the protection and promotion of labour throughout the early twentieth century to the present day. Early labour movement involvement for women was intertwined with a growing suffragette movement and nationalist organisations, though not exclusively.

Arguably the most significant milestone for organised women's labour in the period was the creation of the Irish Women Workers' Union in September 1911. Two weeks prior to the creation of the Union, over 2,000 female employees of the Jacob's Biscuit factory in Dublin withdrew their labour in support of their male counterparts who had gone on strike demanding better wages and other concessions.

Jim Larkin served as the Union's first president, with his sister Delia the first Secretary. The IWWU's role in the 1913 lockout cannot be understated. When the Tramworkers of William Martin Murphy's Tramway's Company walked from their posts on 26th August 1913 in outrage at the company's diktat that no workers were to be members of the Irish Transport and General Workers Union (ITGWU), the most severe labour dispute in Irish history began and action by workers spread like wildfire through the City.

Delia Larkin, somewhat overshadowed by her brother, is a figure who played an unequalled role in terms of women during the Lockout of 1913 and the subsequent years. At the outbreak of the strike, James Larkin went to England in order to seek help and support and Delia Larkin took effective charge in Liberty Hall.

On 1st September 1913 along with the assistance from members of the IWWU, the Irish Women's Franchise League and Inghinidhe na hÉireann, they essentially took on the mantle of feeding and clothing those who were most affected by the turn of events.

She ran the site, which undertook the obligation to feed the union members and their dependants throughout the entire course of the lock-out.

This tremendous project was able to provide three meals daily for up to three thousand children and some of their starving mothers. Liberty Hall was also the site designated for the distribution of clothing which came from sympathetic supporters, largely in Britain; in doing this she was also able to employ some of the women who had lost their jobs. When it was initially theorised by certain circles, that in order to protect the children of Dublin; who bore the brunt of the devastating effects, to move them to houses in Britain to care for them, it was Delia Larkin that they came to for assistance.

Due to the cramped conditions within the Dublin slums that the majority of the strikers had lived in, disease was rife and illness was only exasperated by the near starvation levels experienced by some. It was thought by some that the most humanitarian option was to take the children out the situation. Delia Larkin continued her work in Liberty Hall right up until February 1914.

The build-up to the lockout of 1913 began on 30th August, when the dispute reached Jacob's Biscuit Factory as management posted notices that Union badges were not to be worn on site. When flour had been delivered by a blacklisted firm that had locked out ITGWU workers, three Union men refused to handle it and were summarily dismissed.

By the 1st September, over 300 women did not report for their duties at the factory in an act of solidarity. As the vast majority – up to 60% - of those women were from the Bakehouse, the factory could not function and was closed until, management stated, they could employ replacement workers who were not members of the ITGWU.

On 6th September, the Irish Citizen ran a story that said 'A conflict which suddenly throws out of employment over 600 girls cannot fail to be of deep concern to all who are interested in women's conditions of work'.

IRISH CITIZENS ARMY

During the Lockout, which had spread across the City and had been ruthlessly opposed by the Dublin Metropolitan Police, sympathetic unions in Britain as well as the TUC in Dublin organised food ships to cater for those left bereft during the strike.

Towards the end of September, the first 'food ship' arrived in Dublin to support families. The TUC in London in particular organised and sent food via the SS New Pioneer and SS Fraternity in October to Dublin, and utilised Co-op bakeries in Belfast and Dublin to produce loaves for the workers.

Potentially the most emotive of the circumstances that surrounded the strike, as already mentioned, was the idea of sending starving children to be cared for in England rather than suffer in Dublin. This however, was ferociously opposed by the Catholic Church and the middle class, with particular pressure put upon women by Archbishop Walsh who had said any woman who sent her children away as part of the scheme could not be deemed to be a Catholic mother.

We must not forget the extreme influence that the Catholic Church held over the majority of Irish people at the time, that when they intervened in this way, the idea was essentially over. Senior British socialists such as Dora Montefiore who organised the scheme saw that they were fighting a losing battle. They were forced to abandon most of their plans following the Church's intervention, but not before one last act.

On October 22nd, one of Dora Montefiore's helpers, Lucille Rand brought 50 children to Tara Street baths to be washed and 'clothed with English charity garments', as the Evening Herald described them. Priests from St Andrew's Church in Westland Row led a mob to the baths to protest the action.

The priests declared that they are acting 'on the directions' of the Catholic Archbishop Dr Walsh. Most of the children are prevented from travelling to England and Lucille Rand is arrested on suspicion of kidnapping children. The complaint has been lodged by Josephine Plunkett, the wife of Count Plunkett. One group of 18 children is successfully smuggled aboard the SS Carlow at the North Wall that night.

At an evening rally in Beresford Place, James Larkin declares the clergymen 'a disgrace to their cloth.' He adds that 'the religion that cannot stand a fortnight's holiday in England does not have much bottom or very much support behind it.'

W. M. Murphy's newspapers begin publishing the names of parents who consented to their children participating in what was to be called the 'Dublin Kiddies Scheme'.

Key pillars of support in the City for strikers during the lockout were Countess Markiewicz who along with Delia Larkin had established a soup kitchen at Liberty Hall. Other key figures not just in the labour movement but in the wider nationalist movement throughout this period, like Helena Moloney, aided in the soup kitchens and prepared the basis for women's involvement in wider national issues.

In England, support for the strikers in common with the struggle for women's votes was taken up by Sylvia Pankhurst, daughter of Emmeline, and the federation of the ELFS/WSPU who said of the lockout;

"The Dublin lock-out was to me a poignant incident in our common struggle for a fairer, more humane society. I was glad to accept the invitation [to speak at a supporting event] as an opportunity to show solidarity with the Dublin workers and to keep the women's side of the struggle to the front."

Following 'Bloody Sunday' on 30th August 1913 when police baton charged a workers demonstration, killing one protestor, Larkin and James Connolly proposed the creation of an Irish Citizens Army to protect workers, and was headed by Captain Jack White, an Ulster Protestant and ex-British Army serviceman.

The ICA was revolutionary in more ways than one, as it accepted women openly into its ranks and treated them with equality. Dr Kathleen Lynn for example, as referred to in other sections, was an active member of the ICA and indeed Chief Medical Officer for ICA volunteers during the Rising, and was referred to by Commandant John O'Neill as 'Surgeon General' in his account of the Rising where 200-230 members of the Irish Citizens Army under Connolly took part.

Dr Lynn was accompanied in the ICA by Madeleine French-Mullen and on active service during the Easter Rising. Both were imprisoned together following the insurrection, and were lifelong friends. In 1919 they founded St Ultan's hospital in Ranelagh, Dublin.

J. MCQUAID & E. DOYLE

Alice Brady was a fatality of the heightened tensions, shot dead by a strike breaker in December 1913 apparently accidentally, following a riot in what was then Great Brunswick Street (now Pearse Street).

The lockout ended in early 1914 after calls for a sympathetic strike in Britain fell on deaf ears. William Murphy and the employers had effectively won the bout, and set in motion the devastating downfall of the ITGWU as a result.

No account, even one as brief as this, can refer to the 1913 lockout and the IWWU without referring to Rosie Hackett. She was one of those brave women who, in 1911, withdrew their labour in support of their male colleagues in Jacob's factory.

She was a co-founder of the IWWU located at what is now Pearse Street, where her comrade Alice Brady, aforementioned, lost her life. She led the first IWWU Mayday march in May 1913, and was present to hear Jim Larkin's speech on 'Bloody Sunday'.

Rosie was one of the 300 women who lost their jobs in September of that year for refusing to remove their Union badges. She was a key player in the Liberty Hall food kitchen service for those starving ex-workers who had suffered so terribly during the lockout.

During this time she came into contact with Heleny Moloney and Madeleine French-Mullen, and trained as a printer in the Liberty Hall press, a job she held until long after the lockout. She became a close confidant of James Connolly.

She played her role in the Rising also, working alongside Dr Lynn, with whom she was arrested and held in Kilmainham alongside until her release a few days after the insurrection. She continued her trade union and nationalist activities for many years.

She died on 4th July 1976. In September 2013 it was announced that the new light-rail Luas bridge in Dublin between Marlborough and Hawkins Street, would be named after Rosie Hackett.

Following the internment of a number of high profile women already referred to in this book, the IWWU campaigned alongside other groups to have key female prisoners like Moloney, Carney and Markiewicz released, stating that the reasons some had been held for so long in Aylesbury was because the British were afraid of their influence in the women's labour movement.

BY THEIR VALOUR

The IWWU continued to fight for works rights in post-Independence Ireland, not just for their own female members, who included midwives and nurses but also for men.

The abhorrence of inequality remains a key tenet of the legacy of the early IWWU and the current Services, Industrial, Professional and Technical Union subsumed the IWWU and formed a key part of its equality agenda.

3 REVOLUTIONARY WOMEN

Women were at the front line of social and political upheaval in Ireland and Europe in the early 20th century – not just as supporters of leading men, but as leaders themselves. Their stories are not often told in detail, hampered at the time by Ireland's entrenched patriarchal philosophy.

Nowhere was the role of women so understated, despite its importance, than in the struggle against Britain for Ireland's independence, and in defence of the Union. Whilst women's role in armed insurrection and defence of the Union (in its forms) throughout the 20th century is personified by names like Markiewicz, those who participated in the nation's turmoil over the last 100 years came from many backgrounds and played many roles, all of which should be recognised and remembered.

EASTER RISING AND AFTERMATH

Whilst women were not members – as its name suggests, of the Irish Republican Brotherhood nor the Irish Volunteers, following the completion of IRB plans for the Easter Rising, Padraig Pearse merged Cumann na mBann with the Irish Citizen's Army which also had prominent female members, with the IRB and Volunteers, to become part of the 'Army of the Irish Republic'.

Following the surrender of the Republican forces on Easter 1916, 79 women were arrested[1] (or surrendered) with the men, either as Cumann na mBan or Irish Citizens Army members. They were taken to Ship Street Barracks, then moved to Richmond Barracks on May 2nd where the Courts Martial took place.

[1] Barton, Brian and Foy, Michael 'The Easter Rising' 2011, Page 225

Many of those involved in the Rising such as its leaders were held in Kilmainham Jail were the women were then transferred. A week after the executions of the leaders of the rebellion, all women were released, but 7 were detained. These seven were Countess Constance Markiewicz, Countess Plunkett, Ellen (Nell) Ryan, Marie Perolz, Brigid Foley, Winifred Carney and Helen Moloney.

Winifred Carney (1887-1943) was involved in nationalist, suffragist and trade unionist activities in Belfast. She was secretary of the Textile Workers' Union organising girls working in the mills. She joined Cumann na mBan and was James Connolly's secretary during the 1916 Rising, remaining by his side in the GPO after the general evacuation.

These seven were then transferred to Mountjoy. On 26 June 1916 under the terms of the Defence of the Realm Act (DORA), Carney, Moloney, Perolz, Foley and Ryan[2] were transferred to Lewes Prison in East Sussex which was also used to incarcerate high profile male leaders of the rising like Harry Boland, Thomas Ashe and Eamon DeValera. It should be noted that Lewes is a male prison, not the first time female Irish prisoners had been held in such an environment.

Kathleen Lynn (1874-1955) was born in Cong, Co. Mayo where her father was a Church of Ireland rector. She was one of the first medical graduates from the Royal University of Ireland in 1899, was involved in the suffrage movement and acted as medical adviser when members encountered violence and went on hunger strike.

---

[2] http://hansard.millbanksystems.com/commons/1916/jul/18/miss-ellen-ryans-internment#S5CV0084P0_19160718_HOC_124

Countess Plunkett and her husband were deported to Oxford under Regulation 14B of DORA, while Kathleen Lynn was sent to Bath until she was released from her detention order in August 1916.

Following an announcement from the British Home Secretary on 12 July 1916, 460[3] prisoners including two women were released from prison, the latter being Brigid Foley and Maria Perolz.

Mr Albert Byrne, MP for Dublin Harbour at the time questioned the Home Secretary on the internment of 'lady prisoners' and was duly informed that Foley and Perolz were to be freed[4]. Moloney, Carney and Ryan were then sent to Aylesbury, where they would eventually be joined by Countess Markiewicz on 7th August having been held in Mountjoy until then.

Internment without trial was often used by the British Government, Irish Free State Government and the Northern Ireland Government throughout our chequered history to detain those suspected of being involved in illegal acts against the State.

Internment is defined by the Cambridge Dictionary as 'the act of putting someone in prison for political or military reasons, especially during a war'.

Whilst in the modern era many will look to Operation Demetrius and the 1970's as the primary manifestation of widespread internment on the island of Ireland, that instance is certainly not the first time it has been utilised.

---

3 http://hansard.millbanksystems.com/commons/1916/jul/12/arrests HC Deb 12 July 1916 vol 84 cc320-1
4 http://hansard.millbanksystems.com/commons/1916/jul/12/lady-prisoners HC Deb 12 July 1916 vol 84 c322 [Hansard]

Perhaps the most well-known female Republican in Irish history, Constance Markiewicz was the first woman elected to the British House of Commons (1918) and the first woman in the world to hold a cabinet position as Minister for Labour from 1919-1922. The Countess married Polish aristocrat Casimir Markiewicz, and came from a wealthy landowning family in London.

She played an active role in many National movements in Ireland, the labour movement, the Rising, the first Dáil, opposition to the Anglo-Irish Treaty and the formation of Fianna Fáil.

THE 'GERMAN PLOT'

In April 1918 internment was used against the Sinn Fein leadership, this time as a result of the alleged 'German Plot'. British Intelligence had, on the back of the arrest of Joseph Downling formerly of Casement's Irish Brigade, briefed the British Cabinet and the Dublin Castle Administration of an imminent coup in Ireland with the help of the Germans.

Approximately 150 people were interned and transported to English jails. Countess Markiewicz, Maude Gonne MacBride and Kathleen Clarke were interned in Holloway Prison, London. MacBride was not to be released until October, Clarke was held until February 1919 despite failing health, and the Countess was held until 10th March 1919.

> Defence of the Realm Act (DORA) (and subsequent amending legislation) originally instituted on 8th August 1914 was to legislate for security provisions after the beginning of WW1 but was reconstituted a number of times and granted the Government wide-ranging powers such as internment, land acquisition and censorship. Whilst focussed on the war effort, the Act was used against those involved in the Easter Rising of 1916, particularly Regulation 14B which was used to impose
>
> *'Restrictions on or internment of persons of hostile origins or associations.'*

CIVIL WAR

The 'official' start of the Irish Civil War was marked by the storming of the Four Courts in Dublin by Anti-Treaty forces on 14th April 1922. Article 3 of the Public Safety (Emergency Powers) Act 1923 declared that 'Every person who is now detained in military custody or held as a military prisoner or captive and has not before the passing of this Act been sentenced to a term of imprisonment or penal servitude by any tribunal established by the military authorities, may be detained in custody under this Act' – effectively giving internment a legislative basis in the Irish Free State.

The vivid account of imprisonment by Margaret Buckley in 'The Jangle of the Keys' gives us an insight into the conditions at the North Dublin Union, where female internees were transferred to from Kilmainham on the second week of June 1923, totalling around 270.

"In the second week of June we got word from friendly wardresses [in Kilmainham] that we were to be removed to the North Dublin Union, which was being opened up as a sort of concentration camp for women."[5]

In her book, Buckley describes the conditions in the NDU as 'filthy' and recalls the difficulty Republican Officers had in feeding the inmates at the new complex.

"We now numbered over three hundred, and if I live to be one hundred and twenty I will never forget the job I had as Quarter Master to feed that many on the rations received."[6]

Margaret Buckley was a native of Cork, and a staunch Republican. She took part in the Easter Rising, and was released in 1917, dedicating her time to Sinn Fein. In 1920, she was appointed by Austin Stack as a Dáil Court Judge.

Following her opposition to the Anglo-Irish Treaty, she was interned in both Mountjoy and Kilmainham and went on hunger strike. While interned, she was Quartermaster of Republican Prisoners, and wrote about her experiences in her widely referenced 1938 book 'The Jangle of the Keys'. She was also an organiser of the Irish Women Workers' Union.

In 1934, she was elected Vice President of Sinn Fein.

---

[5] Buckley, Margaret 'The Jangle of the Keys' 1938, Page 47
[6] Ibid, Page 55

> **Kathleen Clarke,** née Daly (1878-1972) was born into a Fenian family in Limerick and earned her living as a dressmaker and shopkeeper.
>
> A confirmed nationalist, she was a founder member of Cumann na mBan. Her husband Tom was active in the Irish Republican Brotherhood (IRB) and the Irish Volunteers and their shop at Parnell Street, Dublin became a centre for IRB activity.
>
> The plans for the 1916 Rising were confided to Kathleen and she was pregnant with her fourth child when both her husband Tom and her brother Ned Daly were executed after the Rising.
>
> She immediately set to work organising the Prisoners' Dependants' Fund to support the relatives of the dead and imprisoned following her release.

There were 323 females held at the Union during this desperate time and several protests took place in the camp due to the number of beds in dormitories, overcrowding and cleaning as well as available rations.

Dormitories had been given pet names such as 'The Devil May Care' and 'Fleming's Hotel' by the women interned there at the time. They shared the complex with 30 female warders and the military at the time.

Scabies, headlice and even serious diseases such as scarlet fever broke out in the camp given the lack of hygiene and problems with medical care and water provision.

In Ann Matthews' 'Dissidents: Irish Republican Women 1923-1941', a source of in-depth accounts and details on the period, an interesting if not harrowing overview of the situation at the Union is provided:

"Between November 1922 and November 1923, 645 women were interned for periods ranging from one or two days to thirteen months.

There were twenty-four separate hunger strikes in Mountjoy, Kilmainham and the NDU, involving 219 women."[7]

On 21st September 1923, General Mulcahy issued an order that all female prisoners should be released. At this time the NDU held 199 women, and Kilmainham held 124.

On 28th September, 79 women were released from Kilmainham, and the remainder transferred to the Union. By 13th October on 98 prisoners resided in the NDU, reducing again to 86 on the 24th October.

51 women went on a hunger strike in October in protest at still being held, lasting until 23rd November when assurances were accepted that they would be freed. By 23rd December all female prisoners as result of the civil war had been released and women were not to be interned by the Southern state again.

WOMEN ON HUNGER STRIKE

The method of hunger strike has been a method of highlighting political grievances and generating publicity to a cause that perhaps would not have received the same amount of attention to the media, or the wider general public.

It also forces the offending government to make a difficult decision, do they allow the prisoner to carry on with their protest, all the while generating more publicity and highlighting the extremes to which they are willing to go to for their causes.

Hunger strike is a long, slow and extremely painful process, which has the potential to make a martyr out of those who undertake this action.

However, they can choose to stop this method of hunger strike, through the quite distressful method of force feeding.

Although the use of hunger strike has been a tool in which Irish Republicans have been long associated with, especially in the 20th century, they were by no means the only group employing the tactic to highlight their grievances against the state.

In the early 1900s hunger strike had been readily used by the suffragette movement across Britain and Ireland. This was most notably a tactic taken up by the leader of the suffragettes, Emmeline Pankhurst who routinely went on hunger strike whilst in prison and was then subsequently, force fed by prison authorities.

In 1913, this led to the introduction by Parliament of The Temporary Discharge for Ill-Health Act (Also known as the "Cat and Mouse" Act). This Act allowed for the early release of prisoners who were so weakened by hunger striking that they were at risk of death.

They were to be recalled to prison once their health was recovered, where the process would begin again. However, as the First World War broke out in 1914, the suffragettes suspended their campaign for the duration of the hostilities.

However, after the Easter Rising of 1916 and during the Irish Civil War, hunger striking again became a popular form of protest in Ireland, and was relatively effective for the women who chose to go down this route.

Between 1916 and 1923, there was a reported 10,000 cases of hunger strike in Ireland of both male and females (although some of these were cases of multiple hunger strikes by the same person).

In 1917, following the Rising, more than forty prisoners went on hunger strike, and were subsequently forced fed.

Mary MacSwiney, whose brother Terence had died on hunger strike in 1920, went on hunger strike herself in Mountjoy Jail in November 1922. She was released after 24 days. Her second hunger strike in April 1923 received noticeably less publicity.

She was imprisoned twice during the Civil War and spent 24 days on hunger strike in Mountjoy in 1922 and 21 days on hunger strike in Kilmainham in 1923. She joined the Munster Women's Franchise League but resigned in November 1914 because of their support for the war effort.

An ardent nationalist, she joined Cumann na mBan, organised their branch in Cork City and served on the national executive. Soldiers arrested her in her classroom in May 1916 and having lost her teaching post because of her political activities, she set up her own school, St. Ita's in Cork.

Her brother Terence, Lord Mayor of Cork, died in Brixton Prison in 1920 after 74 days on hunger strike and Mary embarked with his widow Muriel on a publicity tour in America.

She was TD for Cork from 1921-1927 but abstained from taking her seat in Dáil Éireann as she vigorously opposed the Anglo-Irish Treaty.

Her sister Annie MacSwiney who had fasted outside the prison gates during Mary's first hunger strike began another one herself and was released from prison after 15 days.

Nellie Ryan, sister-in-law of Richard Mulcahy, Minister for Defence, was released after 34 days.

Kate O'Callaghan (1885-1961) née Murphy from near Macroom, Co. Cork was a graduate of the Royal University of Ireland and a teacher. A founder member of Cumann na mBan, she married Michael O'Callaghan who became Lord Mayor of Limerick and was murdered in her presence at their home in Limerick in 1921.

She was elected to Dáil Éireann in May 1921. She opposed the Treaty in 1922 and was elected to the Dáil again in June 1922 but lost her seat in June 1923. During the Civil War she was interned in Kilmainham Jail where she went on hunger strike for nineteen days.

Maud Gonne MacBride was released after 20 days. Maud was interned in Holloway Jail in 1918. She opposed the Treaty, attempted to reconcile the opposing sides in the Civil War and founded the Women's Prisoners' Defence League with Charlotte Despard to help Republican prisoners and their families.

Imprisoned by the Irish Free State in 1923, she was one of ninety-one women who went on hunger strike and was released after twenty days. Privileges withdrawn were restored after a week-long hunger strike by 97 women in Kilmainham Jail where over 300 women were imprisoned in the early months of 1923.

WORLD WAR TWO

The next wave of internment came during World War Two, where in the North, 18 women were detained in Armagh jail alongside ordinary criminals until internment orders were signed. John McGuffin's 'Internment' informs us that twelve were from Belfast, three from Derry and three from Tyrone. We uncovered the names from PRONI documents, but could not find all 18 names.

Nora McKearney	Madge McConville	Mary Keenan
Norah McDowell	Molly Craig	
Agnes McDowell	Norah Ward	
Rosaleen McCotter	Annie T McDaid	
Mary Dempsey	Alice Ashton	
Margaret Agnew	Catherine O'Hara	
Margaret Burns	Teresa Donnelly	

Women were interned during this period, though notably with no public outcry because of censorship imposed under Emergency Powers (Defence) Act 1939 and managed by the Ministry of Information in London which managed propaganda and censored newspapers and other publications under Defence Regulations, thus making campaigning and raising awareness near impossible for the supporters and families of those interned.

Interestingly and in contrast to accounts from internees following Operation Demetrius, relations in Armagh Gaol between those interned during World War two were not always harmonious.

Recently declassified documents from that period show that major disturbances broke out in the gaol on 30th-31st August 1943 because, according to Governor's reports, three Derry prisoners were given their tea by warders prior to the rest of the internees.

A report by the Governor states that he perceived the animosity between the prisoners to be based on a plan by Belfast prisoners to cause an outbreak which the Derry prisoners did not want to be part of, and had requested to be moved to another part of the prison due to bullying by Belfast prisoners as a result. Substantial damage was caused to the internee wing of the prison, and indeed prison warders Joseph Spence and Hannah J Wilson lodged legal cases against a number of prisoners for alleged assaults during that two day period.[8]

Some prisoners had no choice but to 'sign out'. This process involved prisoners physically signing a document that admitted their membership of a specific organisation and that they would not become involved again. Nora McKearney in particular had to sign out due to the financial hardship her family endured while both she and her brother were imprisoned, her brother was being held in Crumlin Road.

POSTWAR PERIOD

During the 1956-61 IRA Border Campaign one woman, Bridie (Bridget) O'Neill was interned. A resident of Norfolk Street in Belfast, her internment documents have been recently declassified by the Northern Ireland Office and show she was interned on 19th November 1959

---

[8] Public Records Office of Northern Ireland, HA/9/2/494A - Misconduct of Internees in HMP Armagh (1943-1944), accessed 4/8/14

BY THEIR VALOUR

following the opinion of the RUC Inspector-General, Sir Richard Pim, who acknowledged the gravity of interning a woman, but stated this 'was only because it is considered to be absolutely essential for the preservation of peace and the maintenance of order'.[9]

The RUC documents list Bridie as a member of Cumann na mBan. She was released by the Minister for Home Affairs on 16th February 1960 at approximately 3:30pm after 90 days in Armagh jail.

The formal internment order for Bridie had to be written on by officials to change 'he' to 'she' and 'him' to 'her', such was the oddity of the powers being used against a female. The documents refer to her as a 'king pin' in a local organisation.

We have included her documents in the following pages, and it is likely that these are the first time they have ever been seen by the public at large. Note the signature of Brian Faulkner on one.

---

[9] Public Records Office of Northern Ireland, HA/32/1/1262A, accessed 4/8/14

INTERNMENT ORDER

WHEREAS it appears to me, on the recommendation of the Inspector General, Royal Ulster Constabulary, that for securing the preservation of the peace and the maintenance of order in Northern Ireland, it is expedient that Miss Bridget O'Neill of 54 Norfolk Street, Belfast,

in the County of the City of Belfast, who is suspected of being about to act in a manner prejudicial to the preservation of the peace and the maintenance of order in Northern Ireland, should be Interned.

Now I, THE RIGHT HONOURABLE W.W.B. TOPPING, Q.C., Minister of Home Affairs for Northern Ireland, by virtue of the powers vested in me by the Civil Authorities (Special Powers) Acts (Northern Ireland, 1922-1943, and the Regulations made thereunder, and of all other powers me thereunto enabling, DO HEREBY ORDER the said Miss Bridget O'Neill

forthwith to be Interned in H.M. Prison, Armagh,

and to be subject to all the rules and restrictions applicable to persons there Interned, and to be kept Interned there until further order.

If the said Miss Bridget O'Neill desires to make any representations against this Order of Internment she should, as soon as may be after a copy of this Order is served on him, hand in a statement of such representations to the official in charge where she is Interned, and such representations shall be duly considered by the Advisory Committee specially appointed for the purposes of Regulation 12 (a copy of which is attached) of the said Regulations.

Dated at Belfast this 19th day of November , 1959.

W. W. B. TOPPING

MINISTER OF HOME AFFAIRS
FOR NORTHERN IRELAND

CERTIFICATE OF SERVICE

A copy of this Order was served by me on the person named herein on the date shown hereunder.

Date of Service: 19/ 11 / 59.

Signature: *m.g. Sennin, D/ Sgt.*

Formal internment order, signed November 1959

Correspondence from Richard Pim, acknowledging the gravity of interning a woman.

Telephone No: Belfast 26421
Our Reference... C.S.14/460
Your ....
Any reply to this communication should be addressed to:
"Inspector General, R.U.C."

HEADQUARTERS
THE ROYAL ULSTER CONSTABULARY
ATLANTIC BUILDINGS
WARING STREET
BELFAST, 1.
NORTHERN IRELAND

13th February, 1960.

Dear Stout,

A few days ago you mentioned to me the case of Miss Bridie O'NEILL who is interned in H.M. Prison, Armagh.

I have had inquiries made by the Belfast police, and attach their report and recommendations.

Having regard to all the circumstances I agree with the course suggested.

Yours sincerely,

Kennedy

W. F. Stout, Esq.,
Ministry of Home Affairs,
Stormont,
BELFAST, 4.

BY THEIR VALOUR

Reference.....................................

<u>Secretary</u>
<u>Minister</u>

  The police have made out a good case for the
internment of Miss O'Neill, and the only point for
decision is whether or not interning a woman is
going to do more harm politically than it would good
operationally.

  We had several women interned during the war
years - generally members of Cumann na M'Ban, but
we have not quite the same free hand today, and must
be more sensitive to possible criticism of our
actions.

  The Inspector General spoke to me this morning
about this case. He is most anxious that the lady
be taken into custody as he feels that she is to a
great extent a king pin in the local organisation.
His information is that further movement of arms or
explosives may be contemplated and that everything
possible should be done without delay that would
disorganise the plans.

  This makes the case for internment much
stronger, and while on balance I think it would be
better if we did not intern women, I recommend that
in this case we do so, but only for a limited period -
say, one month - when she would be released, unless
the conditions then were such that it would clearly
be dangerous to do so.

17th November, 1959

REGIMEAN
Code 18-74

Internal Ministry of Home Affairs memo referring
to Bridie as a 'king pin'

Reference........S.176/330...........

Ministry of Home Affairs,
Stormont, Belfast.

Mr. Stout

Case of Bridget O'Neill, 54 Norfolk Street,
Belfast – Internee

As you are aware, Miss O'Neill was interned on the 19th November, 1959, and was lodged in H.M.Prison, Armagh. The Deputy Inspector General recently had her case reviewed and submitted a recommendation that the police considered that the time had now arrived when she could be released from custody.

The necessary action was therefore taken to effect the internee's release and she was released from H.M. Prison, Armagh, yesterday, 16th February, 1960, at approximately 3.30 p.m.

I have therefore prepared the necessary form of release Order for the Minister's consideration and approval, please.

17th February, 1960.

REGIMEAN
Code 18-74

Internal orders issued for Bridie's release from Armagh Gaol

BY THEIR VALOUR

S.1763

TO THE GOVERNOR, H.M. PRISON, ARMAGH.

I, THE RIGHT HONOURABLE BRIAN FAULKNER, Minister of Home
Affairs for Northern Ireland, hereby order that

BRIDGET O'NEILL

shall be discharged out of your custody as to her internment
under an Internment Order made by the then Minister of Home
Affairs on the 19th day of November, 1959, under Regulation 12
of the Regulations made under the Civil Authorities (Special
Powers) Acts (Northern Ireland), 1922-1943.

Dated this 16th day of February, 1960.

MINISTER OF HOME AFFAIRS
FOR NORTHERN IRELAND
CIVIL AUTHORITY

Official release order from Brian Faulkner

OPERATION DEMETRIUS

On Monday 9th August 1971, Operation Demetrius swung into operation across the North – internment had been imposed by Prime Minister Brian Faulkner and the British Army, informed by RUC Special Branch lists, had set about swooping on unsuspecting citizens.

The outline plan for internment was compiled by HQNI (British Army HQ in Northern Ireland) assisted by the Government Security Unit of the Northern Ireland Government and the RUC.

The arrangements for mass arrests were periodically reviewed by a committee, consisting of representatives of RUC HQ, RUC Special Branch and the Army prior to the operation.

At 11:15am on the day, Brian Faulkner exclaimed that Northern Ireland was 'quite simply at war with the terrorist'. 450 names were on the lists produced by RUC Special Branch for the Army teams to arrest, none of those on the list were known Loyalists, and indeed the information used in the compilation of these lists was out of date and included many who had Republican sympathies, but were not active in the Republican movement at the time.

Of that 450, 342 were arrested, as senior IRA figures had known about the operation in advance and avoided their homes. Internees were processed and held at one of three locations – Long Kesh Camp, Magilligan Camp, or the prison ship The Maidstone docked in Belfast Harbour.

When arrested, detainees were taken to 'Regional Holding Centres' – Ballykinler Weekend Training Centre, Magilligan Weekend Training Centre and Girdwood Park Territorial Army Centre. Some Barracks, such as Town Street and Fort Monagh were used as rendezvous points when distance proved an issue.

Those to be detained after questioning by RUC Special Branch Officers were sent from Magilligan and Ballykinler to HMS Maidstone by Army helicopter. Those held in Girdwood were transferred to Crumlin Road Gaol which was a short distance away.

In total following the 9th August raids, 105 men were released and 237 were detained.[10] By November of that year, 980 men had been arrested.

No women were arrested during the dawn raids, but a considerable number were held during the rest of the period up until 5th December 1975 when internment officially ended under Secretary of State for Northern Ireland, Merlyn Rees.

Elizabeth 'Liz' McKee, a 19-year old Belfast woman, was the first to be interned during the 1971-75 period – on 1st January 1973 for allegedly being a member of the Provisional IRA, as her Detention Order states, 'E Company, 1st Battalion of the Irish Republican Army Provisionals in Belfast' where she is said to have risen to the rank of Adjutant.

A total of 32 women were interned during this period and held in Armagh Gaol. A number of their stories are recorded in 'In the Footsteps of Anne' which is a remarkable collection of memories from those female Republican prisoners who were held in Armagh Gaol.

Life for the internees in Armagh was at times bittersweet. Accounts from 'In the Footsteps of Anne' give us an insight into enduring sisterhood of Republican prisoners. We can piece together the processing of female prisoners when entering Armagh – their story begins with a shower or bath in a freezing cold room with carbolic soap to disinfect, followed by a headlice screening.

A full body search by female prison officers followed, and then a move to one of the wings depending on their status. Armagh catered for Republican internees, sentenced prisoners and 'ordinary prisoners'. Loyalists were also held there, such as the infamous Ann Ogilby murderers, vividly remembered by some Republicans.

---

[10] Report of the enquiry into allegations against the Security Forces of physical brutality in Northern Ireland arising out of events on the 9th August, HMSO, 1971, Chapter 8

J. MCQUAID & E. DOYLE

Their 'rompering' of the single mother contributed to the disbanding of the Women's UDA in the same year. Etta Cowan and Christine Smith were the two senior members of the gang to be imprisoned alongside Elizabeth Douglas.

A unique and harrowing aspect of life for those held in Armagh was how children were to be cared for in the absence of their mothers. Often, grandparents had to step in and take care of their grandchildren, but where that was not an option, prisoners were presented with papers to sign their children over to Social Services, to be placed in the care of the state.

We must also not forget about the often primary role of many of these young women in their householders as main breadwinners. For families who now then had to cope without a family member, the economic impact cannot be understated, and this obviously added to the worries of prisoners.

A particularly poignant testimony from a Republican internee tells of how after release, her young daughter did not recognise her as her mother, and a resumption of 'normal' family life took some time, such was the impact of the estrangement.

Life on the wings for Republican prisoners seems, from the testimonies in 'In the Footsteps of Anne' to be relatively structured. The Republican had an Officer Commanding (OC) in the form of the much-loved and respected Eileen Hickey who oversaw a regime that fostered friendships, but also perpetually upheld the principle of the political nature of their imprisonment, and that of the men in Long Kesh Camp.

In each version of events, jokes about house-proud prisoners who continually cleaned cells are apparent, as well as good humour and a mischievous atmosphere, with inmates playing pranks on each other, especially newcomers. After lock-up at 8:30pm, the women read and replied to letters from family and friends.

"The time in Armagh was one of the best years of my life. I know it sounds strange."[11]

When a woman was committed to the wing, the OC would meet them for a debriefing, to ensure that they had not implicated anyone else inadvertently during interrogation. Then, interestingly, they were given the Standing Orders of the Wing. Official prison rules were largely ignored, but

---

[11] In The Footsteps Of Anne, Geraldine McCann's statement, Page 49

the Republican Standing Orders were sacrosanct.

"I was given the Standing Orders of the gaol. We did not follow the prison rules. It was impressed on us that we had our own rules"[12]

A structured life awaited the Republican prisoners. A command structure akin to that in Long Kesh was in place – an Officer Commanding flanked by an Officer Board comprising an Intelligence Officer, Quarter Master, Training Officer and PRO who met weekly.

The prisoners were subject to cell inspections by the OC every day except Sunday, and drills organised by the Training Officer. Parades were also held monthly, and a cleaning rota and education programme were timetabled by the prisoners themselves – thus the prison authorities had very little input into the daily lives of the women.

In conducting research for this book, one clear reference to fear is widespread. 'Being sent for' by the Governor in Armagh meant that, given the situation both outside the prison and in the male camps, one was to be given news of an injury of a loved one, or worse.

In the time that was in it, worries of those inside were compounded by thoughts about family members, brothers and sisters in particular, who had also been interned. Male internees had been held in Long Kesh, Magilligan and the Maidstone, with men held in Nissan huts under terrible conditions.

The site at Long Kesh which was previously used as an airfield, was hastily constructed and was seen as a short term solution to an expanding prison population as a result of internment. Compounds of huts were put in place for both Republican and Loyalist prisoners. At its apex, 21 compounds littered the site. Up to forty men were held in each hut, with a separate hut for recreation and another for showers and toilets.

The H Blocks themselves were not recommended until the acceptance of the Gardiner Report in 1975. In October 1976, after months of failed negotiations with the Camp management on issues such as food, searches and parole, the camp was set on fire in protest.

---

[12] In the Footsteps of Anne, pg 56, Mairead Taggart's story

A uniform component of criticism has been of the medical support available in Armagh during the internment period. In the mind of a compassionate member of society, one would suppose that medical provision would be readily available and indeed increased for women in a prison environment.

PRISON PROTESTS

The protests that characterised headlines around the world in the 1970's and 80's were reproduced in Armagh by Republican prisoners, with the same, if not more, dedication that those in the Maze and other facilities.

On 15th May 1972, 42 men went on hunger strike in Crumlin Road Gaol led by Billy McKee for political status for both remand and sentenced prisoners alongside internees, who had effective POW status within the prison estate.

> Special Category Status or 'political status' as it was also known, was introduced on 20th June 1972 by then Secretary of State for Northern Ireland, William Whitelaw.
>
> Government papers at the time stated of SCS: 'It sought to distinguish between ordinary criminals and those who found themselves in prison serving sentences arising directly from the disturbed political situation'.

(Source: PRONI, PCC/1/5/7 'Presentation on Prisons: Special Category' 10 March 1976, accessed 19/8/14)

Armagh prisoners followed for 21 days before Special Category Status was granted, political status in all but name. Prior to the introduction, prisoners in Armagh were expected to rigorously conform, including undertaking activities such as cleaning floors in their wing.

Special Category Status ended on 1 March 1976 having been announced in November 1975 by the British Government, in what was seen by Republicans to be the birth of the policy of 'criminalisation'.

Female prisoners were permitted to wear their own clothes unlike those in the Maze, but refused to engage in prison work from 1976 and were heavily punished. This included loss of 50% remission, as well as being locked up for long periods whilst other prisoners worked and had visiting opportunities reduced to one per month with no food parcels permitted.

Numbers on the protest in 1976 was relatively low with five prisoners, but rocketed to almost 40 within three years.

During 1969 Armagh had 9 'political' prisoners. That population exploded by 1976 with over 100 prisoners. Rita Bateson had been only 16 when imprisoned for 3 years, and became the youngest 'non-conforming' prisoner in Armagh.

In March 1978, the 'no wash' protest began in the Maze due to on-going and escalating abuse of prisoners by Prison Officers whilst visiting toilets and showers. The men refused to leave cells to 'slop out' or take showers when requests for in-cell showers were refused by the prison authorities.

When prisoners received news that a prisoner had been badly injured following a fight with a prison officer, and was now in solitary confinement, prisoners responded by wrecking their cells, which prompted the prison authorities to remove all furniture except a mattress and blanket. This was the beginning of scenes of excrement being smeared on walls and urine being poured out of windows and under doors in the H Blocks.

In contrast, the 'no wash' protest in Armagh did not begin until early February 1980 and was provoked by what was described by eyewitnesses as a brutal attack on Shirley Devlin in the canteen area by a Prison Officer.

The Governor had announced a general search of cells whilst the prisoners were eating, as he believed there may be military uniforms being held due to plans to hold a commemoration for a female prisoner's family member who had recently passed.

The protest began the next morning as prisoners had been locked in their cells for 24 hours following the disturbances and it is recorded that Prison Officers would not open the toilet facilities so the prisoners could empty their chamber pots.

Harrowing accounts from 'Only The Rivers Run Free' give us an idea of the gender-specific issues faced by women during their protest;

"Apart from the psychological and hygienic pressure which such a protest engenders, women also have a menstrual cycle to contend with. In Armagh the woman had to state when their period was due, and if it started earlier than anticipated, or came more often than expected, then too bad.

"The women still had to make do with the quota of sanitary towels allocated to them. The fact that they had to sit in their own menstrual blood amidst excreta and urine did not concern the prison authorities."

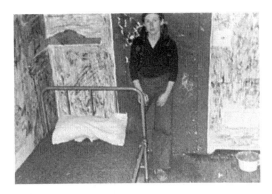

IRA prisoner Mairead Farrell in her cell during the protest, smuggled from Armagh Gaol)

"It was a particularly humiliating form or punishment to ration something so basic and simple as sanitary towels. Yet the governor did precisely that.

He tried to break the prisoners in an exclusively female way."[13]

In an effort to escalate the protest for the re-instatement of 'political status', it was decided on October 1980 that a hunger strike would be commenced in the Maze.

Seven men including Brendan Hughes and Raymond McCartney refused food from the 27th of October until death if the Government did not grant 'The Five Demands':

The right not to wear a prison uniform;
The right not to do prison work;
The right of free association with other prisoners, and to organise educational and recreational pursuits;
The right to one visit, one letter and one parcel per week;
Full restoration of remission lost through the protest.

---

[13] Fairweather et al, Only the Rivers Run Free, Page 222

Mairead Farrell, Mary Doyle and Margaret Nugent started a supporting hunger strike in Armagh on 1st December 1980. The three were moved to a double cell in the prison until news of a solution reached them on 18th December and that Sean McKenna, close to death had been taken off the strike.

When it became clear that the position of the Government was not what was deemed to be 'political status' in the form of the five demands, the H Block and Armagh prisoners expressed their intention to undertake a further strike in a statement in early 1981.

On 1st March 1981, the OC of the prisoners in the Maze, Bobby Sands, commenced his hunger strike. The 'no-wash' protest in Armagh voluntarily ended to allow focus to be given to the second male hunger strike and no female prisoners undertook this strike, though it had been considered by those who had previously engaged in the 1980 strike.

The aftermath of the dirty protest in Armagh, aided by publicity and the work of the National H-Block/Armagh Committee and their local branches, was the widespread increase in interest in and support for women as military assets in the Republican Movement – and inspired the creating of a Women's Department in Sinn Fein in that year.

In a particularly harrowing event in Armagh during the H Block hunger strike, Dolores O'Neill who was Thomas McElwee's fiancé had secured an inter-prison visit after months of talks between her and the prison authorities and visited him on 7th August 1981, the day before he died.

Following the extremely disruptive period at the prison, Governor Hilditch was replaced by a new Governor in Tom Murtagh. Accounts from prisoners at the time vividly remember and place blame squarely on Mr Murtagh for re-introducing a regime of violent – and often random - strip-searching in Armagh on 5 November 1982 after keys to Armagh courthouse had been smuggled into the jail by two remand prisoners in October 1982.

1218 searches were carried out in 1983 with 316 in 1984. After intense discussions within the NIO, and against the wishes of the Governor, random strip searches began on 7 March 1983. An internal report found that as of 19 April 1983, 14 valium and two sleeping tablets were the only items of any concern found during strip searches. Many female prisoners who resisted searches were held in solitary confinement with loss of remission from November 1982.

Kevin McNamara MP, Labour MP for Hull asked a number of probing questions regarding strip searches in Armagh, much to the ire of NIO officials, particularly in 1984. He was a well-known republican sympathizer. He was joined in asking questions in the House of Commons at this time by his colleagues John Fraser, the Member for Norwood and Harriet Harman, the Member for Peckham.

The situation of segregation became a highly charged political issue, with Peter Robinson, then Belfast City Councillor, proposing a motion to the Council calling for separation to be introduced on 16th November 1982. The policy of integration had, prior to the end of the Republican protests on 1st November 1982, meant that Loyalists were in the majority of the integrated wings in Long Kesh and Maghaberry, but at the end of protests, this position was largely reversed.

In October 1982, numbers of female Republican prisoners was somewhat smaller than in previous times, with 40 sentenced prisoners (including two Special Category prisoners), 12 untried, 1 life sentenced prisoner, and two young people held at the pleasure of the Secretary of State.

The female 'No Work' protest was called off on the 1st February 1983.[15]

Of those prisoners, Christine Sheerin, one of the Special Category prisoners, was released on 19th April 1983, leaving one Special Category prisoner, Pauline Deery.

Female population of Armagh jail as on 11 November 1984		
	Sentenced	Untried
Murder	3	
Attempted murder	1	5
Manslaughter	3	
Explosive offences	11	2
Firearms offences	3	
Other offences	1	4
TOTAL	22	11

There is some evidence of female Republican prisoners attempting to implement segregation in June 1982. Documents show that Anne Marie Bateson had been interviewing prisoners in B Wing of Armagh Prison with a view to obtaining voluntary segregation both on the Wing and at work. We have no further information on this attempt, but can assume that it was not successful.

MOVE TO MAGHABERRY

On 18th March 1986 due to the closure of Armagh prison, female prisoners were held at Mourne House in the new Maghaberry Prison outside Lisburn. Only twenty prisoners remained in Armagh. According to Sinn Fein, over 200 strip searches were carried out in the new jail in the first six months of its existence and became a major source of contention, alongside seemingly forced 'integration'.

Accounts from prisoners regarding strip searching encompass a bitter and often violent struggle between prisoners and authorities:

"In 1992 the female prisoners in Maghaberry experienced a horrific forced cell and strip search. On Monday, March 2nd, at 8:20am, the women were told they would not be unlocked because a search of the jail was being conducted. At about 8:30am the male screws (prison officers) walked through the wings singing 'Happy Days Are Here Again'. An hour later the women were told that they would be subjected to a strip search. If they did not comply, they would be put on "report" and "punished". The women refused."[14]

There was no separation between Republicans and Loyalist women in Mourne House, so prisoners shared the facility. A constant battle over rooms and access to facilities between both was a core characteristic of the House. Although there was a small number of loyalist prisoners, and no formal UVF or UDA structures in the jail even into 1990, self-segregation was used by those small numbers, away from Republican prisoners.

Separation in Maghaberry did not occur until 2003 following the Steele Report, and women were transferred from Maghaberry to Hydebank Wood in June of 2004.

---

[14] Gallagher, Philomena 'Women imprisoned as a result of the Struggle' Canadian Women Studies, page 54 Volume 17 Number 3, 1997

[15] Public Records Office of Northern Ireland, NIO/12/323A

PRISONERS SUPPORT AND WELFARE ORGANISATIONS

There were a number of organisations established to support prisoners and their families from the 1919 period through to the 1990's. In the post-Rising period, three core organisations emerged; the Irish National Aid Association, Irish Volunteers Dependents' Fund – established by former internee, Kathleen Clarke, and the London-based Irish National Relief Fund.

Women were central to the fundraising and co-ordinating effort particularly for the Irish Volunteers Dependent's Fund.

"Prior to the Rising, Tom [Clarke] had given Kathleen Clarke possession of some funds, informing her that this money was intended to support the dependents of Volunteers in the aftermath. Along with Sorcha MacMahon of Cumann na mBan, the women's auxiliary to the Irish Volunteers, and John R. Reynolds of the Wolfe Tone Memorial Committee, an IRB front, Clarke drew up an appeal and enlisted the assistance of Cumann na mBan members. Their purpose was to distribute the original funds and raise more."

THE GREEN CROSS AND ORANGE CROSS

In the 'Troubles' era, two primary organisations emerged to support prisoners and their families, divided along community lines. The Green Cross for Republican prisoners, and its Loyalist counterpart, the Orange Cross.

Whilst the Green Cross was more organised and widely spread given the larger numbers of Republican prisoners, the Orange Cross had emerged from the Loyalist community to support UVF prisoners;

"We had no culture or history of prisoners, we started from scratch trying to work out systems...When Gusty Spence went to prison, that was the first time that Loyalists went outside the law. In that era that was the first time a welfare system the 'Orange Cross' was formed. Among working class areas we were the same as the IRA prisoners but once you went outside of those areas you'd no support"

As the prison population rose in that period, particularly for Loyalists, the Loyalist Prisoner Welfare Association was formed which assumed co-ordination of welfare and campaigning responsibility for Loyalist prisoners,

BY THEIR VALOUR

including those women in Armagh Gaol, up until the eventual beginning of the early release scheme in the late 1990's.

FEMALE 'LIFERS'

There were a number of life sentence prisoners held in Armagh during this period, many of them infamous for their actions, including the Price sisters who had blown up the Old Bailey. Some other 'lifers' were held 'at the pleasure of the Secretary of State' - which meant indefinitely due to their age at the time of their imprisonment.

As of 27 October 1980, there were six life sentenced prisoners in Armagh;

Dolours Price – jailed for the bombing of the Old Bailey

Marian Price – jailed for the bombing of the Old Bailey

Ellen Pauline Teresa McLaughlin – held at the Secret of State's pleasure following her role in transporting weapons used to kill a soldier in Shantallow, Derry in October 1974. She also bombed a paint shop and furniture shop in October 1974 and September 1975 and was convicted of membership of the IRA.

Agnes McGreevy – detained for non-conflict related crime

Henrietta Piper Cowan – detained at the Secretary of State's pleasure for the brutal killing of Ann Ogilby, she was aged 17 when she took part in the murder and was a member of the Women's UDA.

Christine Smith – also participated in the murder of Ann Ogilby and detained indefinitely at the pleasure of the Secretary of State. She was 16 at the time of the crime.

FEMALE LOYALIST PRISONERS

It is often believed that no female loyalists served prison sentences. In fact, there were a small number of Loyalist prisoners in Armagh, notably those jailed for the heinous murder of Ann Ogilby who was violently beaten to death with bricks and sticks by loyalist females after Ogilby had an affair with a leading loyalist leader. Ten people had been sentenced for the murder, including Elizabeth Douglas, the leader of the women's UDA unit in the Sandy Row area who ordered two younger members to give Ms Ogilby a punishment beating.

Douglas or 'Lily D' as she was known in Armagh, headed the loyalist prisoners inside the jail. There was a cordial, albeit completely separate relationship between Loyalist and Republican leaders inside Armagh. There was at times acrimony between members of each grouping, but an agreement was reached between both OC's that issues of this nature would be dealt with between them so as not to give the prison officers any entertainment.

Loyalist prisoners both in Armagh and in the Maze benefitted from political status, and undertook their own blanket protest, one notable blanketman of loyalism was the late David Ervine, whilst in the Maze Gusty Spence undertook a hunger strike with 5 others in December 1981 to demand not only special category status but total segregation from Republicans, it ended on 17th December after 5 days.

Interestingly, when Republican prisoners took the Governor and three female Prison Officers hostage in solidarity with the men who had burnt Long Kesh in October 1974, they were joined in that action by UDA prisoners – with the latter even acting against orders from Gusty Spence to stop the action. All women wanted independent assurances that the men of the Maze would not be harmed after their riot.

However, in Armagh given the relatively small numbers of loyalists meant that at times relations were not cordial. In A2 wing for example, because of the often very small loyalist population, there was only one female loyalist on the wing in 1983, and when food was served by Republican prisoners for a time, refused to eat prison food or leave her cell, relying on food parcels.

Following the 1981 hunger strike, Republican prisoners in Armagh began a campaign for total segregation which involved at times wrecking shared educational facilities. Given the large number of Republican prisoners throughout the prison, segregation operated almost in all but name. Orchestrated fights and disorder between both factions pushed for total segregation.

An interesting snippet of the concerns of those administering the Prison Service during the mid-1980's was a record we discovered at the Public Records Office, a briefing to Lord Gowrie about how he could remove the now infamous Monsignor Raymond Murray as Chaplain of

Armagh Prison, as he obviously favoured Republican prisoners and had been causing headaches for the administration outside.

MODERN ERA

Marian Price, sister of late Dolour Price is one of the high profile internees of the modern era. She was released on licence due to the state of her health following her imprisonment for the bombing of the Old Bailey in 1973. She has been forced fed more than 200 times by the prison authorities in Brixton prison during a hunger strike she embarked on with her sister and Gerry Kelly (now SF MLA for North Belfast) a part of demands to be repatriated to a prison in Ireland.

Following the murder of two British soldiers outside Massereene Barracks in Antrim in 2009, she was arrested and questioned. When she held a statement read by a masked man in Derry City Cemetery during a republican commemoration in 2011, she was arrested and charged with encouraging support for an illegal organisation. She was bailed by the Magistrates Court, but the Secretary of State revoked her licence and she was immediately returned to Maghaberry Prison.

She had been held in the former women's wing in the prison in total isolation given Hydebank Wood houses all female prisoners in Northern Ireland. This was due, according to the Prison Service, to her 'category A' status.

The isolation had a profound effect on Marian's mental health, and she was transferred firstly to the hospital wing of Hydebank Wood, and then the mental health unit in Belfast City Hospital. She was released following the reinstatement of her licence in May 2013, just over two years after she had been imprisoned.

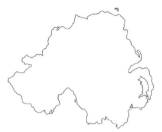

4 WOMEN AS DEFENDERS OF THE NORTHERN STATE

The British state suffered heavy losses throughout the period 14th August 1969-31st July 2007 which we would classify as the beginning of the 'Troubles' until the end of the British Army's Operation Banner, i.e. their role in supporting the police and civil authority in Northern Ireland.

Three strands of operational organisations fall into the category of 'State forces' for the benefit of this chapter; the British Armed Forces, Royal Ulster Constabulary and Northern Ireland Prison Service. Some Paramilitary groups regarded members of these services as 'legitimate targets'.

BRITISH ARMED FORCES

One feature of research particularly into those female members of the British Army who died during Operation Banner has been that it is extremely difficult to compile a complete list of those who lost their lives. Many local Army memorials are incomplete, and some did not have a single female name inscribed on them, which is very disappointing. Many UDR memorials do refer to the 'men and women' who served, but many do not show the names of the fallen. Details of all Armed Forces deaths are included in the Appendices.

Whilst conducting the research for this chapter, the UK Ministry of Defence was asked to outline the number of female military personnel deaths during Operation Banner broken down by Regiment or Corps, but could not provide names of the deceased. This is detailed in Table 1.

Table 1: UK Armed Forces[1] female deaths[2] as a result of operations in Northern Ireland, 14 August 1969 to 31 July 07

Corps	Total female deaths	Operation Banner	Outside NI
All	26	24	2
Intelligence Corps	1	1	0
Queen Alexandra's RANC	1	1	0
Royal Army Medical Corps	1	1	0
Royal Irish Regiment	2	2	0
Ulster Defence Regiment	13	13	0
Women's Royal Army Corps	8	6	2

Source : Defence Statistics (Health)
Notes:

1.　　　Figures are for in-Service UK Armed Forces regular and reservist personnel only and do not include any ex Service personnel who may have been targeted by Terrorists.

2.　　　Figures are for all causes of death; Hostile action, accidents, assaults, coroner confirmed suicide and open verdicts, natural causes and cause not known.

3.　　　Deaths that occurred outside of NI but were deemed to be the result of Irish Terrorism.

4.　　　Formed 1 July 1992 when the Ulster Defence Regiment merged with The Royal Irish Rangers.

5.　　　Formed 1 August 1970 and disbanded 30 June 1992.

In addition to Operation Banner, the Royal Navy carried out Operation Grenada and Operation Interknit between 1983-85 by patrolling both the Irish Sea and in Interknit's case, Carlingford Lough to stop smuggling, arms transfers and general criminality.[16]

The Royal Navy lost 26 members during the Troubles as a result of paramilitary action, including 21 Royal Marines killed.

Royal Marines of 40 Commando also played a role on land in at different times of tension in 1983 and 1984 particularly in South Armagh.

The Armed Forces utilised a large range of resources for Operation Banner, These included helicopters, aircraft, sea-going vessels (both military and operational, e.g. HMS Maidstone used as a prison ship), armoured vehicles, tanks, troop carriers, bases, observation posts, force protection resources, bomb disposal equipment and much more. The Royal Air Force lost 4 members due to paramilitary activity.

An FV1611 Humber 'Pig'

---

[16] Roberts, John 'Safeguarding the Nation: The Story of the Modern Royal Navy', Barnsley 2009

It is worth noting that despite the death toll of women in Northern Ireland who were members of the British Armed Forces, women have only recently been given the option to join an Infantry Unit.

COVERT OPERATIONS

In contrast to women being unable to serve in the infantry, some did serve with elite units such as 14 Intell (14 Field Security and Intelligence Company) – sometimes known as 'The Det' or alongside the Special Air Service (SAS) in different roles. 'The Det' was a successor to the infamous Military Reconnaissance Force or MRF that had infiltrated the IRA in the early 1970's before being stood down as a result of its cover being blown.

The MRF operation operating out of a laundry in Belfast was the first such covert operation to have a women directly involved from the Armed Forces. During the early 1980's a troop of SAS soldiers was attached to the Det, forming Intelligence and Security Group (NI).

All covert Army operations in Northern Ireland were overseen and directed by the Head of the RUC Special Branch. As part of the training undertaken by what were volunteers from across the Army, MPK5 submachine gun , browning pistols, maps, cameras and cars were amongst the armoury of gadgetry employed, with backup from the RAF when required.

Sexism against raised its head even within these highly trained units, with frequent references to it in 'She Who Dared: covert operations in Northern Ireland with the SAS' by a female operative and author. Examples of this range from women being able to leave the Det and join SAS troops, to the requirement that women must have partners during operations, which men were not subject to.

Women, such as the author of the above publication were decorated for their service in the Det, but for many the only path they could follow after their covert operations, was in the Intelligence Corps, which involved little field work.

14 Intelligence and Security Group

NORTH

Based in Derry

SOUTH

Covered Fermanagh, Tyrone, Down and Armagh

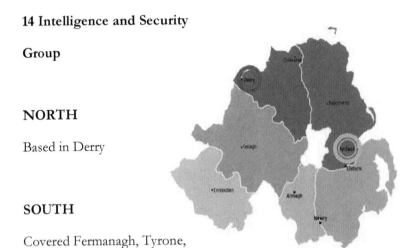

PERCEPTION BY THE PUBLIC

On deployment to Northern Ireland as a result of increasing sectarian violence, soldiers were greeted as protectors by a large section of the Nationalist community. However, within a short period of time, the Army were seen to be working alongside the RUC and other agencies which were seen to be upholding Unionist rule, and the warm welcome soon became a frosty hatred.

Particularly after the Falls Curfew and other now notorious events, the Army and its personnel became targets of abuse and violence, and surrounded by controversy which is well documented.

FEMALE SERVICE PERSONNEL WHO LOST THEIR LIVES

After extensive research we believe we have identified all female members of the Armed Forces who lost their lives in Operation Banner. These proved difficult to verify and near impossible to confirm due to the lack of co-operation from the Ministry of Defence. Every effort has been made to correctly identify the soldiers/officers in question.

There were numerous assaults and attacks on members of the RUC and the Prison Service in the conduct of their duties, and numerous members of the Army were wounded, however it is possible that this is one of the primary instances where a definitive list of female RUC, Prison Service and Army members who were killed have been compiled in one place.

We contacted the MOD regarding the Palace Barracks Memorial Garden and the names listed therein in order to corroborate our lists, but we were instead directed to speak to a veteran who voluntarily managed the garden who wished to discuss a fee for the information, we declined.

BY THEIR VALOUR

Intelligence Corps
Capt Henrietta Louise
De-Haga Steele-Mortimer

**Royal Army Medical
Corps**
Captain Janis Mary Cant

UDR
L/Cpl Jean Leggett
Pte Margaret A. Hearst
Pte Eva Martin
Cpl Heather C. J.
Kerrigan
W/Pte Mary Elizabeth
Karen Cochrane
W/Pte Hilary
Ann Gaynor
W/Cpl Ciara Alexandra
Ousby
W/Pte Heather Elizabeth
Sloan
W/Pte Constance Evelyn
Beattie
W/Pte Sandra Brown
W/Pte Belinder Rose
Gillespie
W/Pte Hester Shields
Sgt Gertrude Myrtle
Cathcart

**Royal Women's Army
Corps**
W/Pte Ann Hamilton
[Guildford bombings]
W/Pte Caroline Slater,
[Guildford bombings]
L/Cpl Roberta Thain.
L/Cpl Judith Ann
Pattison
W/Pte Karen
Roberta Cowan
W/Pte Maria Anne
Hornsby
W/Cpl Elaine Marrison
W/Sgt Alison
Sybil Stryker
W/Pte
Kathryn Waterland

**Royal Irish Regiment
(Home Service)**
L/Cpl Caroline Mary
Crawford
Maj Joyce Gillison MBE
[d. 2002]

**Queen Alexandra's
Royal Army Nursing
Corps**
Cpt Lynda Maureen
Smith

MEMBERS OF THE NI PRISON SERVICE

Two female members of the Prison Service were killed in the conduct of their duties by paramilitaries, both serving at the women's prison in

Armagh. Prison Officers were primarily targeted during periods of high tension within prisons, when protests were on-going and paramilitary groups specifically targeted officers to exert influence on the service itself and the conditions prisoners were held in. Images below from the NPIS Roll of Honour.

Mrs Agnes Jean Wallace was killed on 19th April 1979 by the Irish National Liberation Army (INLA), she was forty years of age and is believed to have been shot by a sniper outside the prison facility.

Another serving member of staff that had been indirectly killed by a paramilitary group was 26 year old Elizabeth Chambers who was struck by a car driven by an off-duty UDR member who had been shot by a sniper. She was killed on the 7th October 1982.

ROYAL ULSTER CONSTABULARY

Six female members of the RUC were killed in the conduct of their duties, one as young as nineteen years of age. All were killed by paramilitary groups directly. Women had served in the RUC since 15 November 1943 following a directive during the World War Two. Over 300 RUC officers were killed during the Troubles.

ROYAL ULSTER CONSTABULARY

Female RUC officers were not routinely armed until 1994, and around that time they numbered less than 2,000. They served with considerable threat to their lives, and many were killed in the line of duty.

Detective Constable Ivy Kelly who was 29 was killed alongside Rosemary McGookin when Newry RUC Station was the subject of a mortar attack on 28th February 1985.

Colleen McMurray was killed on 27 March 1992 by the Provisional IRA when her armoured vehicle was destroyed by a mortar attack in Newry. She was 35 years old.

Tracy Doak was 21 when she was killed by a remote controlled bomb in Killeen, Co Armagh on 20th May 1985, she was 21.

Rosemary McGookin, 27 was killed on 28th February 1985, when a mortar was fired at the Edward Street RUC barracks in Newry.

Linda Baggley died on 2nd June 1976 at the age of 19 nine days after being shot by the IRA in Derry whilst on foot patrol in Chapel Road.

Mildred Harrison was 26 when she was killed when a bomb exploded on 16th March 1975 in the Ormeau Arms Bar in Bangor as her patrol passed. She was 26.

A woman of note within the RUC is Cathleen (Kate) Carlisle who joined the Royal Ulster Constabulary in 1963, rising to the rank of Superintendent, the first woman to do so. She retired in 1995 as a sub-divisional commander.

UDR 'GREENFINCHES'

Whilst written records of the experiences of female soldiers from Regiments based in Britain who served in Northern Ireland are widespread, we will focus on the story of female members of the Ulster Defence Regiment or UDR, who were fully integrated into the Regiment unlike many of their counterparts in Britain, but only after a Bill had been passed in the House of Commons lifting the ban on women serving in the UDR which was part of the Hunt Report.

The name 'Greenfinch' comes from their callsign which was initiated by Brigadier Harry Baxter.

The UDR was created by Parliament in 1969 following passage of the Ulster Defence Regiment Act which received Royal Assent on 18th December of that year after the Hunt Report recommended the disbandment of the Ulster Special Constabulary (B -Specials) to be replaced by a reserve RUC force and a local part-time Army regiment.

The UDR had full and part time members, but uniquely, Greenfinches had to submit a form of permission from their husbands prior to joining – something I doubt female members of the IRA or UDA would have considered.

A primary tenet of the Greenfinches in the UDR was the searching of women suspects by women, something men could not do, and thus directly targeting a source of personnel that was increasingly being utilised by the IRA in particular.

Societal change too impacted upon the role of women in the UDR and wider afield. Until 1990 when a European Court ruling outlawed the practice, members of the Armed Forces who became pregnant were automatically dismissed. Again in contrast to some special category prisoners who actually gave birth and were allowed to keep their newborns with them in prison for up to a year, Greenfinches suffered gender discrimination.

WOMEN IN THE LOYAL ORDERS

Contrary to popular belief, women have played an active and fruitful role in Orange Order since the 1880's. It is difficult to find official records of the foundation of what became known as the Association of Loyal Orangewoman in Ireland, but unofficial sources refer to the founder being the Hon. Helena de Moleyns, wife of the then North Armagh MP, Colonel Edward Saunderson.

The order lapsed and was re-established in 1911, with the Association of the present day being formed with consent of the Grand Lodge of Ireland by Mrs. R. H. Johnstone of Bawnboy, County Cavan. It is believed its first meeting was held in 12 Rutland Square, Dublin in February 1912.

The ALOI is affiliated to the Grand Lodge of Ireland, and conducts its own parades and marches. It rose to prominence in the modern area due to its activity during the Drumcree dispute where many of its members protested.

The ALOI is well regarded within the Loyal Orders, and a song (composer unknown) was penned to commemorate their contribution.

BY THEIR VALOUR

Ladies Orange Lodges O!

The Orange cause is booming strong

Since ladies joined the Order O
They gain large numbers all along
From centre to the border O.

Long live the lasses O!
Long live the lasses O!

Our Ulster girls shine bright as pearls

Arrayed in blue and orange O.

For love of country and of creed
They crowd round William's banner O

From James and priests their sires he freed

To his immortal honour O.

Long live the lasses O!
Long live the lasses O!
The Orange movement's doubly strong

Upheld by Orange lasses O.

And thus throughout all Ulster wide

In townships and in cities O

The ladies lodges come to bind
And lilt their orange ditties (songs) O.

Long live the lasses O! Long live the lasses O!
No Jesuits plot nor bishops' rape
Can stop the Orange lasses O

Each lodges' centre is a light Of loyalty and progress O

To work 'gainst those who love the night

And hate the British Empire O.

Long live the lasses O! Long live the lasses O!
So every day let's sing and pray
God speed the Orange lasses O

Long live the lasses O Long live the lasses O

So everyday let's sing and pray
God speed the Orange lasses O!

A BBC Documentary entitled 'Sisters of the Lodge' was aired in March 2011.

5 CASE STUDIES

Dolours Price

Dolours Price was born 21 June 1951, sister of Marian and daughter of Albert, two prominent Republicans in West Belfast. She was convicted as one of the eight volunteers who bombed the Old Bailey, New Scotland Yard and the British Forces Broadcasting Office in London on 8th March 1973 which injured 200 people. She was joined in the operation by her sister and by Gerry Kelly, now SF MLA for N Belfast.

Both Price sisters attended St. Mary's Teacher Training College where Dolours studied the Bachelor of Education course.

She is believed to have led the Old Bailey operation, and was picked up with the rest of the team at Heathrow Airport on their way back home, before the bombs exploded.

She was sentenced to life for each charge, commuted to 20 years. Both Dolours and her sister Marian went on hunger strike in Brixton Prison in November 1973 demanding to be transferred to a prison in the North.

During her incarceration, and throughout the 200 days she engaged in a hunger strike, Dolours and Marian were force-fed until the end of their strike in June 1974. The process was described by Marian during an interview;

BY THEIR VALOUR

"Four male prison officers tie you into the chair so tightly with sheets you can't struggle, you clench your teeth to try to keep your mouth closed but they push a metal spring device around your jaw to prise it open.

"They force a wooden clamp with a hole in the middle into your mouth. Then, they insert a big rubber tube down that. They hold your head back. You can't move.

"They throw whatever they like into the food mixer - orange juice, soup, or cartons of cream if they want to beef up the calories. They take jugs of this gruel from the food mixer and pour it into a funnel attached to the tube.

"The force-feeding takes 15 minutes but it feels like forever. You're in control of nothing. You're terrified the food will go down the wrong way and you won't be able to let them know because you can't speak or move. You're frightened you'll choke to death."

As part of the campaign to have Marian and Dolour repatriated, their father Arthur ran in the 1974 Westminster election as an Independent for West Belfast, coming third with 11.9% of the vote.

In 1975 as a result of the IRA truce, Kelly, Hugh Feeney and the Price sisters were transferred to Irish jails. The Price sisters, who were held in Durham Prison at the time, were transferred to Armagh Gaol. They were both released in 1980 and 1981 respectively.

In 1983, Dolours married Stephen Rea in Armagh Cathedral, officiated by Raymond Murray, Chaplain of Armagh Gaol and life-long friend. They had two sons, and separated in 2003.

As the 'peace process' was progressed by the Sinn Fein leadership, the Price sisters openly criticised the path that was plotted and the contents of the Good Friday Agreement.

In recent times, Dolours publicly referred to her role as the driver in the disappearance of Jean McConville, allegedly under the orders of Gerry Adams, who has always denied his involvement in the IRA.

Between 2001 and 2006 Dolours and prominent Republican Brendan Hughes participated in an oral history project at Boston University where she is believed to give an account of her involvement in the McConville murder and the IRA.

The PSNI have subpoenaed the tapes, which were not to be released in the participants lifetimes.

It is believed that since the breakup of her marriage, Dolours suffered with alcohol and medication problems.

She was found dead at her home in Malahide, Co Dublin on 24 January 2013 and was buried in Milltown Cemetery on 28th January. She died an unrepentant Republican.

Wendy Millar

Wendy Millar, of 'Queen of the UDA' as she was known for some time, is a founding member of the Ulster Defence Association, and a founder of the UDA's first women's unit in the Shankill area of West Belfast.

She was a staunch supporter of C company 'Brigadier' Johnny 'Mad Dog' Adair and faced expulsion from Northern Ireland by the UDA following a feud within Loyalism. She was seen as a senior member of the organisation, which is unusual for a female in a loyalist paramilitary group.

Judith Gillespie

Judith Gillespie served as Northern Ireland's most senior police officer from 2009 until her retirement in 2014.

She joined the then-RUC in 1982 as a constable, and served as the Acting Chief Constable until Matt Baggott was appointed in 2009. She is a graduate of Cambridge University and of the FBI's National Executive Institute.

She had twice been rejected to join the Royal Ulster Constabulary because of her gender, but quickly rose through the ranks.

Following the implementation of the Patten Report, Gillespie had the option of taking severance estimated to be around half a million pounds, but rejected this to continue her work with the PSNI.

She was the first woman to reach chief officer status in the PSNI.

She was made an OBE in the Queen's 2009 Birthday Honours and then upgraded to a Commander of the British Empire in 2014.

6 PEACEMAKERS

Women played a pivotal, if often overlooked, role in creating a lasting peace on the island of Ireland. This included community representatives, politicians, prisoners and ex-prisoners

On 31st August 1994, the IRA announced a 'complete cessation of military operations' which paved the way for talks on the future of Northern Ireland in a constitutional framework. This followed the secret talks between John Hume and Gerry Adams leading to the Hume/Adams Initiative in 1993 on creating a peace process in the North.

"We are mindful that not all the people of Ireland share that view or agree on how to give meaningful expression to it. Indeed, we do not disguise the different views held by our own parties.

As leaders of our respective parties we have told each other that we see the task of reaching agreement on a peaceful and democratic accord for all on this island as our primary challenge."[17]

The Loyalist paramilitaries responded seven weeks later with their own ceasefire announced by Gusty Spence on behalf of the Combined Loyalist Military Command.

---

[17] Joint Statement from John Hume and Gerry Adams, 24 April 1993

BY THEIR VALOUR

The TUAS (Tactical Use of Armed Struggle) document outlined the Republican movements' strategy post-ceasefire, which was used as a basis for discussion within Sinn Fein, the IRA, with prisoners and stakeholders.

This strategy was criticised by some, like Brian Keenan, but there is no evidence to suggest female prisoners or female members of the Republican Movement rejected the premise and direction of the document.

A major Republican women's conference was held in Belfast in March 1994 by Clar na mBan, bringing together a wide range of women to discuss the progression of the peace process and women's role in it.

Whilst there was an absence of Protestant/Loyalist organised debate on the issues raised by the conference, one issue from the report of the Clar na mBan conference was clearly articulated – a male-dominated peace and a male-dominated process was not what the women of Northern Ireland wanted.

"The danger is that once again we [women] are going to be asked to bury our demands, this time in the common purpose of achieving peace."[18]

The concensus around the outcome of the deliberations by women in conferences and discussions around their input to the peace process followed a relatively common thread.

"I think women should have more say in the running of the country because it's men ruined it. Men are just a necessary evil. They are all self-centered and selfish."[19]

May Blood, now Baroness Blood, then chair of the Shankill Women's Forum said when addressing a meeting of the newly formed NIWC in May 1996:

"On the one hand, women are seen – by both men and women themselves – as the 'backbone of the community' and the potential peacemakers who can leave their differences aside and talk to each other. On the other hand, it is the very concerns on which women have found common cause which appear to be excluded from the current debates in Northern Ireland. Women – celebrated as the peace makers – have been

---

[18] Clar na mBan 'A Women's Agenda for Peace: Conference Report' pg 9

[19] Fairweather et al 'Only the Rivers Run Free, Northern Ireland: the Women's War' Pg 286

largely absent from the 'peace process.'"[20]

WOMEN AND THE ISSUES

Decommissioning, All-Party talks and prisoners became major issues for not just Nationalism, but for loyalist representatives during in the 1995-1996 period. The loyalist community were particularly keen on keeping their prisoners on board for discussions and the direction they were taking, but we have found no evidence of discussions undertaken with female Loyalist prisoners in Maghaberry at the time.

Another critical issue that came to the fore in the 1995-1996 period on the streets of Portadown was the Drumcree march, and led to the emergence of female community leaders such as the SDLP's Brid Rodgers who was continually at the forefront of the dispute urging progress and a settlement to the divisive issue.

Her famous television scene on 11th July 1996 when the RUC forced through the Orange Order march down the Garvaghy Road, stating in exasperation 'this is an outrage!', firmly placed her in the hearts and minds of residents in the area, and the wider consciousness of Nationalists throughout the North at the time.

The IRA called off its ceasefire on 9th February 1996, and talks began in June of the same year.

A major risk was taken by the British Government by calling elections for talks on May 30th 1996 using a list system. An interesting feature of

---

[20] Sales, Rosemary 'Women Divided: Gender, religion and politics in Northern Ireland' pg 195

these elections were the numbers of female candidates, and those elected to the talks.

Party/Candidate list name	Females elected
SDLP	1
DUP	0
UUP	0
SF	2
Alliance	1
UK Unionist Party	0
Progressive Unionist Party	0
Ulster Democratic Party	0
Northern Ireland Women's Coalition	2
Labour	0

(Source: Northern Ireland Elections)

With almost 100 candidates across the region vying for election, it is clear women played a major role in the pre-emptive negotiations and must have also played a significant role internally in their respective organisations/groups.

The Forum and the multi-party talks were two heads of the same beast. In order to become a representative at the talks, one had to be elected to the Forum. The Forum itself was established 'for the discussion of issues relevant to promoting dialogue and understanding in Northern Ireland' as established by the Northern Ireland (Entry to Negotiations, etc) Act 1996.

The Act outlined that entry to the talks – without specifically making reference to Sinn Fein – was linked to 'unequivocal restoration of the ceasefire in August 1994.'[21]

Lucilita Breathnach was elected to the talks for Sinn Fein, and was part of its negotiating team with the British Government, one of a small number of women to participate at such a high level. Eileen Bell of Alliance who was part of the talks went on to become the Speaker of the Northern Ireland Assembly.

---

[21] Para 9 Cm 3232 'Northern Ireland: Ground rules for Substantive All-Party Negotiations' HMSO 1996

(Lucilita Breathnach outside Downing Street during the talks)

Dorita Field, the single female SDLP talks member, was originally from South Africa. She became the Party's Treasurer and was the first Nationalist Belfast City Councillor for the Balmoral Ward, she passed away in 2004.

Monica McWilliams of the NI Women's Coalition later become the Chief Commissioner at the NI Human Rights Commission in 2005.

The SDLP walked out of the Forum in July 1996, but remained at the talks.

OPSAHL COMMISSION

What was to be known as the Opsahl Commission began as 'Initiative 92's Citizen's Inquiry' and aimed to harness the views of the ordinary man and women on the future of Northern Ireland. 3,000 submissions were made and then analysed by a team headed by Norwegian human rights lawyer Professor Torkel Opsahl.

For the first time on an official basis, the view of the citizens of the jurisdiction were compiled without the input of politicians, and the views of women were particularly interesting.

"They articulated their ability as Catholic and Protestant women to co-operate and work pragmatically on the issues that affect their lives, counterposing their efforts against those of politicians who did not do so."[22]

Politicians in Northern Ireland rejected the report and its findings, which concluded that neither self-determination or majority Unionist rule should be the way forward for the region, but that 'parity of esteem' represented the best way forward. It was significant in that it demonstrated the willingness - and impatience on the part of the women of the jurisdiction to progress peace in a way men seemed unable to – with equality and co-operation.

"In their evidence to the Commission women attributed much of their sense of exclusion and powerlessness to the lack of debate about ordinary, everyday policy issues. It was as if these issues at the very centre of their lives had been disregarded and deprioritised by politicians."[23]

THE PEACE PEOPLE

The Peace People is an organisation still in existence today, and was formed in August 1976 following a tragic incident in Belfast that claimed the lives of a young IRA member Danny Lennon, and three young children who were hit by his car as he lost control of after he was shot by a British patrol in the Finaghy Road North area.

Betty Williams, a local resident, having been petitioned by local women in the area for an end to violence spontaneously after the terrible event, and Mairead Corrigan, sister in law of Anne Maguire, mother of the children who had been killed, met on August 13th at the BBC studios in Belfast for the first time.

Mairead made an empassioned plea for an end to violence on television. On 14th August, a cross community rally and march was held at the scene of the deaths of the Maguire children, and people walked to Milltown Cemetery. Sources say up to 10,000 people attended the march.

The Community of Peace People, or simply The Peace People, was formed and led by the two women and Belfast journalist Ciaran McKeown.

---

[22] Hinds Bronagh 'Women working for peace in Northern Ireland' in Galligan Y, Ward E and Wilford R 'Contesting Politics: women in Ireland North and South' pg 112

[23] Ibid pg 112

It's stated aims, through a declaration, were:

"We have a simple message to the world from this movement for Peace. We want to live and love and build a just and peaceful society. We want for our children, as we want for ourselves, our lives at home, at work, and at play to be lives of joy and Peace. We recognise that to build such a society demands dedication, hard work, and courage. We recognise that there are many problems in our society which are a source of conflict and violence. We recognise that every bullet fired and every exploding bomb make that work more difficult. We reject the use of the bomb and the bullet and all the techniques of violence. We dedicate ourselves to working with our neighbours, near and far, day in and day out, to build that peaceful society in which the tragedies we have known are a bad memory and a continuing warning."

It organised marches, lobbied politicians both in Ireland, the UK and America, and attempted to capitalise on the emotional and psychological hurt of the people in both communities with a view to bringing it to bear on those involved in violence.

It did not have universal support. Leaders of a march through the Falls Road on 23rd October 1976 were attacked by Republicans. Two memorable rallies were held and widely attended, one at Trafalgar Square in London, the other at Boyne, Drogheda. After these high profile marches and rallies, the organisation of the Peace People changed at the focus of the three leaders pulled in different directions.

Mairead Corrigan and Betty Williams were honoured by the Norwegian Nobel Committee in 1976 as recipients of the Nobel Peace Prize.

NORTHERN IRELAND WOMEN'S COALITION

In 1995, the UN held their Fourth World Conference on Women in Beijing. The Beijing Declaration and Platform for Action both focus on women's empowerment and equality.

"Equality between women and men is a matter of human rights and a condition for social justice and is also a necessary and fundamental prerequisite for equality, development and peace. A transformed partnership based on equality between women and men is a condition for people-centred sustainable development. A sustained and long-term commitment is essential, so that women and men can work together for

BY THEIR VALOUR

themselves, for their children and for society to meet the challenges of the twenty-first century."[24]

Those principles of equality, development and peace were key themes that formed the raison d'etre of the Northern Ireland Women's Coalition which was established only weeks prior to the Forum Talks in 1996 – some of whose members had been at the Conference.

The Coalition was just that, a group of women that did not encourage uniformity from its members, it rather encouraged difference of political identity.

It was built on the shoulders of women groups in the community and at the coal face of community development. Those women involved realised that women needed to have an input not just into the political future of the region, but also in the social and economic future.

The European dimension of the work being undertaken by some of the groups involved in women's conferences that led to the formation of the

Coalition fed the belief that co-operation and a strong sense of social justice was a pre-requisite for the Coalition if it was to make real progress as a political entity.

"Although women at the grassroots level do not agree on a single analysis of the Northern Ireland conflict, they share a strong commitment to resolving differences and reconciling the many rich traditions in Northern Ireland."[25]

The Coalition was born into what many would describe as 'the deep end'.

It was formed only a short period prior to the 1996 Forum Talks election, where it ran 70 candidates across the North and because the electoral system used for these elections was a list system, a threshold was determined to elect delegates.

---

[24]United Nations Entity for Gender Equality and the Empowerment of Women 'Report of the Fourth UN Conference on Women' Beijing, 1995

[25] Hinds Bronagh 'Women working for peace in Northern Ireland' in Galligan Y, Ward E and Wilford R 'Contesting Politics: women in Ireland North and South' pg 115

The NIWC did not have any of its candidates elected, but it passed the threshold for delegates and was awarded two seats at the Talks which were taken by Monica McWilliams and Pearl Sagar.

"It was the answer of women and men, to the refusal of political parties to make any serious effort to ensure women a place in negotiating constitutional change."[26]

The two representatives took their seats at the talks, but encountered severe criticism for briefing excluded parties such as the Ulster Democratic Party and Sinn Fein, both who had been excluded because their linked paramilitary groups had broken ceasefires and as such they breached the Mitchell Principles of non-violence which were sacrosanct for entry to the talks.

The Coalition insisted on focussing on the inner workings of the talks themselves. They secured change in the standing orders of the negotiations, forcing parties to secure agreement on proposals from participants rather than simply other parties.

They also constituted a working group of the four smallest groups at the talks to consult on key issues and to troubleshoot issues that they all had an interest in, acting as a counter to the numbers of the larger parties.

If we look at the achievements of the NIWC at the talks, we need only to look to the Civic Forum. It was the Coalition who insisted on the inclusion of a counterweight to the powers of political parties in the Assembly, by giving civic society a voice and particularly – one could deduce, women.[27]

Following the Agreement and referenda, the 1998 elections to the new Northern Ireland Assembly saw the Coalition return two MLA's – Monica McWilliams for South Belfast and Jane Morrice for North Down. The organisation stuck to its guns on community designation, and its Members signed the Member's Book as 'cross community' at the first sitting of the new Assembly. It also had a Councillor elected in the 1997 local government elections.

---

[26] Ibid pg 124

[27] Vikki Bell, In Pursuit of Civic Participation: The Early Experiences of the Northern Ireland Civic Forum, 2000-2002, Political Studies, vol 52 pp 565-584

Unfortunately both Members lost their seats in the 2003 Assembly election, and whilst the organisation itself continued to have a public profile, it was wound up in 2006.

It could be argued that the participation of the Women's Coalition in the Forum talks spurred the other established parties to include more women in their organisations and in senior level positions going forward. However, it could also be argued that the Women's Coalition was a mish-mash of women, who genuinely wanted women's participation to be highlighted, but got lost in the age old acrimony between politics based on ethnic division that exists here.

MO MOWLAM

Arguably the biggest shift in the fragile process at this time was the election of a Labour Government in London on 1st May 1997, and the appointment of Marjorie (Mo) Mowlam as Secretary of State, the first woman to hold the post.

The politically astute MP for Redcar had previously been the Shadow Secretary of State and was well across her brief. The new Government clearly prioritised the peace process in their opening months in power, evident by Tony Blair's visit to the region 15 days after the election, and behind-the-scenes diplomacy that helped produce the new IRA ceasefire on 20th July 1997 which enabled Sinn Fein to enter into the peace talks after accepting the Mitchell Principles on 9th September.

Interestingly, the wording of the statement from the IRA announcing the ceasefire matches exactly that of the British Government Command Paper which outlined ground rules for entry to multi-party talks –

'unequivocal restoration of the ceasefire of August 1994'.

Months before the Labour victory in 1997, Mo was diagnosed with a brain tumour which was kept hidden until the British press began to publicly draw attention to her appearance in the form of hair loss from chemotherapy and radiotherapy treatment.

Although Mo only served as Secretary of State for two years from 1997 until 1999, it was an extremely progressive yet cautious period for the peace process and one which many agree was aided by her approach and bravery.

"She had a rapport with the general public - she wasn't a stuffy, suited politician, but a real person and she came across very much that way."[28]

In February 1998, Mo undertook one of the best remembered and courageous actions of any British politician in relation to the peace process. Loyalist prisoners in the Maze withdrew their support for the peace process on 3rd January, threatening the entire enterprise.

On Friday 9th February, as she had announced a few days earlier, Mo engaged with Loyalist prisoners inside the Maze prison and facilitated a reconsideration of their support by reassuring the men that concessions were not being made to Republicans.

"The size of the risk Mo Mowlam took when she went into the Maze on the Friday can be appreciated from the nature of the men she met in the prison's tatty gynasium. She talked to five members of the Ulster Defence Association, including Michael Stone, the gruesomely tattooed multiple killer responsible for one of Northern Ireland's most horrific atrocities in 1988 when he used guns and grenades on mourners at the Milltown cemetery."[29]

Interestingly during this immense flurry of consultation with prisoners, it was claimed that female Loyalist prisoners in Maghaberry were not consulted by their own organisations.

"The male prisoners have been consulted, but the women have not been asked. No-one has been up to the women's prison to ask them what they think. Women prisoners are not given the same respect. They are mainly in there for supporting men."[30]

From March 1998 until the Agreement reached in April, Prime Minister Tony Blair engaged more in the talks, at the expense of the Secretary of State. From early 1998, UUP Leader David Trimble, who had no personal rapport with Mo, wanted direct contact with the Prime Minister, which

---

[28] Sir Reg Empey speaking on Mo Mowlam's death, 19th August 2005, BBC

[29] Rawnsley, Andrew 'Servants of the People: The Inside Story of New Labour' Page 303

[30] Sales, Rosemary 'Women divided: gender, religion and politics in Northern Ireland' pg 200

undermined the authority of Dr Mowlam, who he saw as being too close to Nationalists.

The post-Agreement period was one of acrimony between the Secretary of State and her Prime Minister. At the Labour conference in 1999, Mo received a standing ovation for her work in the North during the leaders speech, and columnists were lauding her as a possible Prime Minister of the future which caused friction between her, the Prime Minister and his senior staff.

"But I knew I didn't want to leave N. Ireland, although now I was increasingly realising that my position had been made untenable – I had been undermined to the point that even if Tony had decided to keep me there the counter-briefing had made it impossible for me to do the job."[31]

When in October 1999 she was removed from the Northern Ireland post and re-assigned to the Cabinet Office, Mo made no secret of her displeasure. She was replaced by Peter Mandelson, who was close to Tony Blair.

"I felt frustrated about leaving N. Ireland at such a crucial stage in the peace process."[32]

In a further demonstration of her estrangement with the Labour leadership, her personal security which many previous Secretaries of State retained long after leaving Belfast, was removed in January 2000.

Dr Mowlam died in 2005 after a fall at home.

PRESIDENT DR MARY MCALEESE

Mary McAleese (nee Lenaghan) served as the Eighth President of Ireland from 1997-2011. Born in Belfast, and the first holder of the Office from the North, she played an enormous role in bringing peace and stability to the island of Ireland.

She succeeded Mary Robinson (first female Irish President) both as Reid Professor of Criminal Law, Criminology and Penology at Trinity College in

---

[31] Mowlam, Majorie 'Momentum; The Struggle for Peace, Politics and the People' pg 286

[32] Ibid pg 347

Dublin and as Ireland's Head of State. She served as Queen's University's first female Pro-Vice Chancellor.

President McAleese, despite criticism from opponents prior to her election who felt she would be a divisive figure on the issue of Northern Ireland, set the theme of her Presidency as 'building bridges'. Eoghan Harris, a vociferous critic of McAleese in the run up to the 1997 election, referred to her as a "tribal timebomb".

Her dedication to reconciliation was evident following many trips to Northern Ireland, and receiving many guests of all traditions to the Phoenix Park throughout her term in office. She had experienced the Troubles first hand as her family, from Ardoyne, were forced to leave their homes due to intercommunal violence.

President McAleese, alongside her husband Martin, forged a relationship with Protestants and Loyalists in the North by holding 12th of July events at the President's Residence and working with former UDA leaders such as Jackie McDonald with whom she had a good relationship.

When asked in a recent interview by Boston College about her work towards reconciliation, she said:

"My view was, God put me here for a purpose: to stand my ground and make genuine peace with those from whom we were estranged. You have to invest in building, and maintaining, friendships because we are all neighbours — Loyalist, Republican, Protestant, Catholic — and we aren't going anywhere. The Good Friday Agreement gave us the political framework for peace and reconciliation, but on a day-to-day basis there is still much work to be done in building up that trust. We build to fill the centuries' arrears, as the poet John Hewitt said."[33]

Whilst it would be easy to focus on a range of initiatives by the President that fostered trust and respect across Ireland, one initiative that brought the UK and Ireland closer together in a hitherto unimaginable forum, was spearheaded by the President.

---

[33] Smith, S, The Boston College Chronicle, 14/11/2013 (http://www.bc.edu/publications/chronicle/FeaturesNewsTopstories/2013/top-stories/q-a--mary-mcaleese.html)

On Thursday 27th May 1993, Mary Robinson made the first ever official visit to the British Monarch in London. President McAleese went further, she visited London a number of times and had a cordial relationship with Queen Elizabeth. Almost 18 years to the day of the first official meeting between the Heads of State of the UK and Ireland, Queen Elizabeth, at the invitation of the President made a three day official State Visit to the Republic of Ireland.

This had been the first time a British Head of State had visited the Republic in its history, the last visit being a century earlier in 1911 by the Queen's grandfather George V.

In a highly symbolic visit, the Queen and President paid tribute to fallen soldiers of World War I and II, but crucially, visited the Garden of Remembrance in Dublin, created in dedication of those who fought against the British for Ireland's independence. The visit was hailed by many as the new beginning to Anglo-Irish relations.

The groundwork laid by both female Presidents led to Ireland's current President, Michael D Higgins, engaging in a State Visit to the UK, the first of its kind. During her visit to Northern Ireland as part of her Diamond Jubilee, the Queen shook hands with former IRA Commander and deputy First Minister in the Northern Ireland Executive, Martin McGuinness.

President McAleese led the way in terms of non-political relationship building in Ireland and the UK, and is widely recognised as one of Ireland's most successful Heads of State. She is currently studying for a doctorate in Canon Law in Rome.

WOMEN POST-AGREEMENT

Female Republican prisoners in Maghaberry endorsed the Agreement prior to the Referendum. As part of the Early Release Scheme, seven women in total were released six of those in 1998, according to NIO documents.[34]

Strand One, paragraph thirty three of the Agreement made provision for a 'Civic Forum' to be made up of voluntary, civic and business leaders from across Northern Ireland. A gender balance was required for all representative groups, a small victory for the Women's Coalition. The

Forum met from 2000 until the suspension of the Assembly in 2002, but it has not been reconstituted since the restoration of the Assembly in 2007.

[34] Northern Ireland Office, Freedom of Information Request, Ref: 14/161

The NI Life and Times Survey of 1999 asked how individuals voted in the 1998 Referendum. 72% of female respondents, whilst only a microcosm of the wider female constituency, voted 'Yes' to men's 71%. In 2002, a special supplement to the Survey asked 'The women's movement has been important in improving women's situation in Northern Ireland' with almost 50% of all respondents, male and female, agreeing with this statement. The respondents were also clear that women should get involved in politics to address issues that concern them.

In the first Executive, two women were appointed by their parties as Ministers – the SDLP's Brid Rodgers as Agriculture Minister and Sinn Fein's Bairbre de Brun as Minister for Health.

Following the death of David Ervine in January 2007, Dawn Purvis became Leader of the Progressive Unionist Party – the first female party leader in Unionism apart from a short period in the UUP's history.

Women had slowly but surely begun to hold high office and positions of responsibility not only in public life generally, but also within their respective organisations.

Republican female ex-prisoners were prioritised by Sinn Fein after the signing of the Agreement. Individuals like Martina Anderson, Jennifer McCann, Carál Ní Chuilín and Mary McArdle have all served as important figures both internally in their respective parties and in public life after their release from prison.

Anderson, McCann and Ní Chuilín have all served in Ministerial roles since 2007, whilst Mary McArdle went on to become a Special Adviser to Ní Chuilín as Minister for Culture, Arts and Leisure despite being the Minister's superior in Republican prison structures.

ANTI-AGREEMENT WOMEN

A number of high profile women such as Marian Price broke away from mainstream political organisations in protest at the Agreement, whilst in the political arena Arlene Foster and Norah Beare defected from the UUP to the DUP in protest, although this wasn't until 2004.

Marian Price and her sister Dolours had become poster girls of the Republican movement in the seventies after bombing the Old Bailey.

They had undertaken hunger strikes and suffered severe illness whilst in prison and endured force feeding. They were incarcerated alongside Gerry Kelly, all of who campaigned to be repatriated to Irish jails during their imprisonment.

Of the Agreement, Marian stated:

"In 1974 the Sunningdale Agreement was a much stronger agreement and offered much more to republicans and nationalists, than the Good Friday Agreement and it was rejected outright by the republican movement. And there was a war fought for thirty years after that. After having rejected Sunningdale, to accept the Good Friday Agreement and suggest that that was what the war [was for], it's criminal."[35]

Marian went on to become a high-profile member of the 32 County Sovereignty Movement, an anti-agreement Republican organisation.

Another high profile opponent of the Agreement was Peggy O'Hara, mother of hunger striker Patsy of the INLA who stood in the 2007 Assembly election on an Independent Republican ticket in Foyle against well-known Sinn Fein members Raymond McCartney and Martina Anderson. She polled a very respectable 1,800 votes in the constituency but was not elected.

Maire Og Drumm, daughter of former SF Vice-President Maire Drumm who was murdered on 28th October 1976 is an active member of Eirigi, a Republican Socialist organisation that has rejected the Good Friday and St Andrews Agreements.

Eirigi states of the Agreements that they are:

"convinced that these two most recent treaties are considerably more likely to solidify British rule in Ireland than they are to end it"[36]

WOMEN IN LEADERSHIP IN THE PRESENT DAY

Whilst there are many women who hold senior positions both in the political arena and elsewhere, it is important to recognise the women currently holding senior positions within the Northern Ireland Assembly, and their respective parties as a testament to the work of the women's

---

[35]English, Richard 'Armed Struggle: The History of the IRA' pg 317

[36]Eirigi, 'Imperialism – Ireland and Britain' 2007

movement since the formation of the Women's Coalition in pushing gender equality in a predominantly male profession, and putting pressure on parties to prioritise women and women's issues.

At the present time, there are thirty female Members of the Northern Ireland Assembly out of a possible 108, up from 20 at the 2011 election. Whilst a relatively small number, the female members across parties are vocal, effective and have rising profiles.

Margaret Ritchie, MP for South Down for the SDLP succeeded Eddie McGrady both in his Assembly and Westminster seat. She had begun her career as a Councillor for the Party in 1985, and rose to become the first women to lead the SDLP, she also held a Ministerial post for the party in Social Development.

Maeve McLaughlin is a former MLA for Foyle, succeeding Martina Anderson when she replaced Bairbre de Brun in the European Parliament. She served as Chair of the key Health Committee at Stormont, responsible for holding the Health Minister to account and is a former Leader of Sinn Fein on Derry City Council. She lost her seat in the May 2016 Assembly election.

Carál Ní Chuilín is a former Republican prisoner and current MLA for North Belfast for Sinn Fein. She was promoted to the post of Minister for Culture, Arts and Leisure in 2011 and served until 2016.

Jennifer McCann is another former prisoner. She represents West Belfast for Sinn Fein and was a Junior Minister in the Office of First and Deputy First Minister, responsible for supporting deputy First Minister, Martin McGuinness in his wide portfolio. Jennifer was arrested aged 20 for shooting a member of the RUC and sentenced to twenty years.

Megan Fearon is one of the youngest Members of the Assembly, representing Newry and Armagh. She was elevated to the position of Junior Minister in the new Executive Office in May 2016.

Arlene Foster is the most senior female member of the Northern Ireland Executive, serving in a number of Ministries before taking over the DUP in 2015 and becoming First Minister. She is a Democratic Unionist Party MLA for Fermanagh and South Tyrone. Arlene was originally elected in 2003 as an Ulster Unionist, but defected a year later to the DUP with Jeffrey Donaldson and Norah Beare. During a short period from 11 Jan

BY THEIR VALOUR

2010 until 3rd February 2010 she made history when she served as Interim First Minister when Peter Robinson stepped down in the wake of the Iris Robinson scandal.

Michelle Gildernew stunned the Ulster Unionist Party in 2001 when she took the Westminster seat of Fermanagh and South Tyrone with a 53 vote majority. She went on to become Agriculture Minister from 2007 until 2011, and in the 2010 UK General Election, she held her seat by 4 votes against a United Unionist candidate. She lost her seat in the UK General election of 2015.

Michelle O'Neill is the current Minister for Health. She is a Sinn Fein MLA for West Tyrone and was Dungannon and South Tyrone Borough Council's first ever female Mayor in 2010-11. She also served as Agriculture Minister until May 2016.

Dolores Kelly is a Deputy Leader of the Social Democratic and Labour Party. She had been an MLA for Upper Bann from 2003- 2016, succeeding Brid Rodgers. Another record setter, Dolores was the first Nationalist Mayor of Craigavon in 1999. She also represented the SDLP on the Northern Ireland Policing Board and was the Party's Social Development Spokesperson.

Anna Lo is a former Alliance MLA. She was elected to the Assembly in 2007 representing South Belfast. Anna is the first member of an ethnic minority elected to the Assembly, and was awarded an MBE in 1999 for her work for the Chinese migrant community.

Anna did not contest the 2016 Assembly election and has said she was close to leaving Northern Ireland after racist abuse from loyalists in 2013-4. She was the Alliance candidate for the European Parliament in the 2014 election, polling over 44,000 votes.

Catriona Ruane succeeded Martin McGuinness as Minister of Education in 2007 and has been a Sinn Fein MLA for South Down since 2003. She gained prominence in the public arena as Education Minister by scrapping the 11+ academic selection exam. She is currently the Principal Deputy Speaker of the NI Assembly.

Dawn Purvis was a PUP MLA from the death of David Ervine in 2007 until the 2011 election when she lost her seat. Dawn was the first female leader of her party, but resigned from the PUP in June 2010 citing the party's continued links to the increasingly violent UVF. She is a former Northern Ireland Director for Marie Stopes.

Ann Travers has been a campaigner for justice for victims of the conflict, and came to prominence in 2011 after Mary McArdle, a former female member of the Provisional IRA who had played a role in the murder of her sister Mary, and the attempted murder of her father, a judge, was appointed as a Special Adviser to then Sinn Fein Culture Minister Caral Ni Chuilin.

Ms McArdle was jailed for her part in the 1984 atrocity, but released under the terms of the Good Friday Agreement. Ann learned of the appointment via the press, and launched a campaign to have the Special Adviser step down. Backed by TUV Leader Jim Allister, the saga caused a media storm, with Sinn Fein standing accused of insensitivity over the appointment.

We interviewed Ms Travers in 2014. Her continuing focus on victims and the need to address the legacy of the past has put her in the frontline of reconciliation and justice efforts, and like many women before her, she had taken on the current establishment in her own way, to seek justice for her sister.

When you raised concerns about the appointment of Mary McArdle as Special Adviser to the DCAL Minister, did you feel there was widespread support from the community to question the appointment?

On the 18th of May 2011 at about 10.05 am I received a phone call from a BBC researcher for BBC Radio Ulster Talkback, asking if I had seen the front of the Irish News, I hadn't so she told me that Mary Ann McArdle, the only person convicted of my sister's murder and attempted murder of our parent's had been appointed as Special Adviser to the SF Culture Minister.

These roles are commonly seen as "gifted" positions. They are funded by the tax payer so my elderly mother was in the bizarre position of contributing towards her daughter's murderer's salary. Just hearing Mary McArdle's spoken by someone outside of our family was like I had been punched long and hard in the stomach.

I spoke on Talk Back that day and so the media blitz began, not done intentionally but fell that way. I felt so desperate that my sister's memory was being trampled on I hoped that if SF saw and heard me they would re-think.

BY THEIR VALOUR

Mary McArdle would move to a position funded by SF and not the tax payer. I must say here I believe and my father very much believed in the reintegration of ex-prisoners, everyone deserves a second chance especially if remorseful, however I also believe that they must carry a duty of care and a mindfulness towards their victim.

When I started to speak out the tsunami of support was amazing as was the abuse from some republicans including SF councillors. When visiting my mother on a weekend and leaving church on a Sunday people would approach me and say "well done, you are saying just what we want to say".

I would be stopped while in the supermarket. I received hundreds of message of support on social media, emails, letters and phone calls.

I also received abuse "you're a celebrity victim" tweeted one now SF Councillor from North Belfast, no understanding just how hurtful that was, I never wanted to be a victim in the first place, least of all one having to speak up for her sister. "Your Dad deserved it......he was part of a corrupt judiciary. .....he was a cog in an orange state." "your sister was a Brit" "hell rub it up you". Just a few examples.

However the vast majority of people supported me and asked me not to stop. I was giving them a voice.

In terms of the legacy of the peace process, did you feel the appointment had ignored the principles of reconciliation?

Yes I did. It took no thought into consideration for victims' families and especially how it may affect our victim. We had no prior notice or consultation. There was no mindfulness, duty of care, consideration or respect for my sister's human rights. No thought or consideration for the re-traumatisation it would cause.

As a woman, did you feel your contribution was respected as equal?

Yes, I did absolutely. I think when I was lobbying and politicians met me they realised I just wasn't "a little woman" but someone determined that innocent victims Human Rights are of equal importance to those who made them victims in the first place.

In terms of the current setup in the Assembly and Executive, do you feel there is a focus on real reconciliation and respect for either tradition?

I certainly believe that nobody wants to go back to how it was "never again". I do believe however to have true governance and accountability there must be an opposition.

As a woman, do you feel there are fundamental problems with the current setup in the Executive and Assembly in terms of addressing the past?

I feel the humanity of it is often forgotten about, as are the real lived experiences. It is difficult for those who have been hurt to trust politicians if there is a constant air of whataboutery. In my opinion, there is no fixed solution.

Each family and individual must be treated as the unique individuals that they are. The principles though must remain the same; Mindfulness of language, compassion, genuineness, respect, no whataboutery.

It has often been said that women find it easier to engage in reconciliation and progressive moves towards peace, do you agree?

Perhaps this is said because of the belief that women like to talk and are open about their emotions. It doesn't frighten them. However in the past few years I have met many compassionate men, both politicians and lay people, so no I don't strictly agree with this, I've also met some hard, stubborn women! I believe it's down to personality and how much you don't judge or justify but put yourself in the others shoes.

7 APPENDICES

We have included some appendices of information from the UK Ministry of Defence about the deaths of soldiers from Operation Banner that have some relevance to our work.

APPENDIX 1

Table 1: UK Armed Forces deaths due to Road Traffic Accidents on Operation Banner by regiment and year of death, 14 August 1969 to 31 July 2007, numbers

Regiment	All	1969	1970	1971	1972	1973	1974	1975	1976	1977	1978	1979	1980	1981	1982	1983	1984	1985	1986	1987	1988	1989	1990	1991	1992	1993	1994	1995	1996	1997	1998	1999	2000	2001	2002	2003	2004	2005	2006	2007
All	236	2	3	8	12	13	10	12	13	10	10	7	5	11	3	4	11	13	3	9	5	6	3	4	5	1	1	7	1	5	2		1			1	2	1
Royal Navy	2														2																									
Royal Marines	3				1						1											1																		
Household Cavalry	1			1																																				
The Blues and Royals (Royal Horse Guards and 1st Dragoons)	1			1																																				
The Royal Armoured Corps	11			2			1	2	1	1	2	1	1																											
The Royal Scots Dragoon Guards (Carabiniers and Greys)	1							1																																
9th/12th Royal Lancers (Prince of Wales's)	1					1																																		
14th/20th King's Hussars	1			1																																				
The Royal Hussars (Prince of Wales's Own)	1					1																																		
13th/18th Hussars (Queen Mary's Own)	3						1			2																														
15th/19th The King's Royal Hussars	1							1																																
17th/21st Lancers	1		1																																					
Royal Tank Regiment	1							1																																
Royal Regiment of Artillery	8			1	1	1																																		
27th Medium Regiment	1					1																																		
45th Medium Regiment	1				1																																			
102nd (Ulster) Air Defence Regiment (Volunteers)	1			1																																				
Not known	1				1																																			
Corps of Royal Engineers	9		1				1	1		1		1		1		1	1	1																						
Royal Corps of Signals	6									1		1								1									1										1	
Infantry	159	2	3	4	9	8	5	7	8	5	7	3	4	4	5	2	1	10	10	2	6	8	5	6	3	3	3	1	1	6	1	4	2		1		1	1	1	1
Grenadier Guards	2															2																								
Scots Guards	3								1													1																		
Welsh Guards	1																			1																				
The Royal Scots (The Royal Regiment)	1											1																												
The Royal Highland Fusiliers	1																													1										
The Gordon Highlanders	2				1				1																															
The Argyll and Sutherland Highlanders	4								1																				3											
The Queen's Regiment	1		1																																					
The King's Regiment	1								1																															
The King's Own Royal Border Regiment	2																											1	1											
The Queen's Lancashire Regiment	2							1																					1											
The Royal Regiment of Fusiliers	3				1		1				1																													
The Royal Anglian Regiment	3		1										1	1																										
The Green Howards	1																																1							
The Duke of Wellington's Regiment (West Riding)	4				3												1																							
The Cheshire Regiment	1																														1									
The Worcestershire and Sherwood Foresters Regiment	2																		2																					
The Staffordshire Regiment	1																														1									
The Royal Welch Fusiliers	1																													1										
The Royal Regiment of Wales	2			1											1																									
The Royal Irish Rangers	4		2	1																											1									
The Ulster Defence Regiment	82		1	6	3	5	6	7	4	2	6	1	3	2	4	2	1	6	9	1	6	5	2	2																
The Royal Irish Regiment	16																			2	1	2	1	1		2		4	1								1	1		1
The Parachute Regiment	4		1								1																													
The Gloucestershire Regiment	2						2																																	
The Royal Gloucestershire, Berkshire and Wiltshire Regiment	1																											1												
The Duke of Edinburgh's Royal Regiment (Berkshire and Wiltshire)	1																													1										
The Light Infantry	5						2	1						1														1												
The Royal Green Jackets	8	2																						3	1															
Army Air Corps	3								1			1					1																							
Royal Corps of Transport	6			1	1		1	1		1	1																													
Royal Army Ordnance Corps	6					2	1					1																												
Royal Pioneer Corps	2				1																																			
Army Catering Corps	3		1								1																													
The Royal Logistic Corps	1																															1								
Royal Army Medical Corps	1													1																										
Corps of Royal Electrical and Mechanical Engineers	3				1				1	1																														
Adjutant General's Corps	11			2	2		1	1		1			1	1	1				1																					
Intelligence Corps	3						2																	1																
Royal Air Force	6		1						1	1					1																									

Source: Defence Statistics (Health)

BY THEIR VALOUR

APPENDIX 2

Table 1: UK Armed Forces1 non hostile2 deaths as a result of Operation Banner by regiment and cause, 14 August 1969 to 31 July 2007, numbers

Regiment	All	Natural Causes	Accidents (exc RTA)	Assaults	Suicide or open verdicts[3]	Cause not known
All	483	144	209	12	73	45
Royal Navy	1	0	1	0	0	0
Royal Marines	2	0	1	0	1	0
Army	462	139	201	12	65	45
Household Cavalry	1	0	0	1	0	0
The Blues and Royals (Royal Horse Guards and 1st Dragoons)	1	0	0	1	0	0
The Royal Armoured Corps	7	2	5	0	0	0
The Royal Scots Dragoon Guards (Carabiniers and Greys)	1	1	0	0	0	0
4th/7th Royal Dragoon Guards	1	0	1	0	0	0
9th/12th Royal Lancers (Prince of Wales's)	0	0	0	0	0	0
14th/20th King's Hussars	0	0	0	0	0	0
The Royal Hussars (Prince of Wales's Own)	0	0	0	0	0	0
13th/18th Hussars (Queen Mary's Own)	0	0	0	0	0	0
15th/19th The King's Royal Hussars	2	0	2	0	0	0
17th/21st Lancers	2	1	1	0	0	0
Royal Tank Regiment	1	0	1	0	0	0
Royal Regiment of Artillery	15	3	7	0	5	0
3rd Regiment Royal Horse Artillery	1	0	0	0	1	0
4th Regiment	1	0	0	0	1	0
5th Heavy Regiment	1	0	1	0	0	0
27th Medium Regiment	0	0	0	0	0	0
32nd Heavy Regiment	1	0	0	0	1	0
40th Regiment	1	0	0	0	1	0
45th Medium Regiment	1	1	0	0	0	0
49th Field Regiment	2	1	0	0	1	0
102nd (Ulster) Air Defence Regiment (Volunteers)	1	0	1	0	0	0
Not known	6	1	5	0	0	0
Corps of Royal Engineers	19	4	11	1	3	0
Royal Corps of Signals	13	4	6	0	3	0
Infantry	345	114	139	8	39	45
Grenadier Guards	3	0	1	0	2	0
Coldstream Guards	3	0	2	0	1	0
Scots Guards	7	2	3	0	2	0
Welsh Guards	0	0	0	0	0	0
The King's Own Scottish Borderers	4	0	4	0	0	0
The Royal Scots (The Royal Regiment)	2	1	1	0	0	0
The Royal Highland Fusiliers	0	0	0	0	0	0
The Black Watch	2	0	1	0	1	0
The Gordon Highlanders	1	0	1	0	0	0
The Queen's Own Highlanders	3	0	3	0	0	0
The Highlanders (Seaforth, Gordons and Camerons)	1	0	0	0	1	0
The Argyll and Sutherland Highlanders	2	0	2	0	0	0
The Queen's Regiment	2	1	0	0	1	0
The Royal Hampshire Regiment	2	0	1	0	1	0
The Princess of Wales's Royal Regiment	3	0	1	0	2	0
The King's Regiment	2	1	1	0	0	0
The King's Own Royal Border Regiment	3	0	2	0	1	0
The Queen's Lancashire Regiment	2	1	0	0	1	0
The Royal Regiment of Fusiliers	3	0	3	0	0	0
The Royal Anglian Regiment	5	0	4	0	1	0
The Prince of Wales's Own Regiment of Yorkshire	4	1	1	1	1	0
The Green Howards	0	0	0	0	0	0
The Duke of Wellington's Regiment (West Riding)	5	0	3	0	1	1
The Cheshire Regiment	1	0	1	0	0	0
The Worcestershire and Sherwood Foresters Regiment	1	0	0	0	1	0
The Staffordshire Regiment	2	0	1	1	0	0
The Royal Welch Fusiliers	1	0	0	0	1	0
The Royal Regiment of Wales	1	0	1	0	0	0
The Royal Irish Rangers	1	0	1	0	0	0
The Ulster Defence Regiment	208	88	71	5	2	42
The Royal Irish Regiment	43	16	13	0	13	1
The Parachute Regiment	11	1	8	1	1	0
The Gloucestershire Regiment	0	0	0	0	0	0
The Royal Gloucestershire, Berkshire and Wiltshire Regiment	0	0	0	0	0	0
The Devonshire and Dorset Regiment	1	0	1	0	0	0
The Duke of Edinburgh's Royal Regiment (Berkshire and Wiltshire	0	0	0	0	0	0
The Light Infantry	5	0	3	0	2	0
The Royal Green Jackets	11	1	6	0	3	1
Army Air Corps	7	0	6	0	1	0
Royal Corps of Transport	6	1	4	0	1	0
Royal Army Ordnance Corps	3	0	2	0	1	0
Royal Pioneer Corps	4	1	3	0	0	0
Army Catering Corps	3	0	3	0	0	0
Royal Army Pay Corps	2	1	1	0	0	0
The Royal Logistic Corps	7	1	3	1	2	0
Royal Army Medical Corps	4	0	2	0	2	0
Corps of Royal Electrical and Mechanical Engineers	9	4	0	1	4	0
Adjutant General's Corps	12	4	7	0	1	0
Royal Army Vetinary Corps	1	0	0	0	1	0
Intelligence Corps	3	0	1	0	2	0
Queen Alexandra's Royal Army Nursing Corps	1	0	1	0	0	0
Royal Air Force	18	5	6	0	7	0

J. MCQUAID & E. DOYLE

Source: Defence Statistics (Health)
Notes:
1.	Figures are for regular and reservist personnel.
2.	Excludes Road Traffic Accidents (RTA).
3.	As confirmed at a coroner's inquest.

Table 2: UK Armed Forces1 non hostile deaths as a result of Operation Banner by year of death and cause, 14 August 1969 to 31 July 2007, numbers

Year	All	Natural Causes	Accidents (exc RTA)	Assaults	Suicide or open verdicts[3]	Cause not known
All	483	144	209	12	73	45
1969[4]	4	1	2	0	1	0
1970	9	3	3	1	1	1
1971	8	1	4	0	1	2
1972	24	3	14	0	2	5
1973	22	7	13	1	0	1
1974	20	6	8	1	0	5
1975	25	8	12	1	0	4
1976	21	5	13	0	0	3
1977	15	5	9	0	0	1
1978	15	8	6	0	1	0
1979	27	9	8	1	2	7
1980	20	5	14	0	0	1
1981	16	3	11	0	0	2
1982	16	8	4	1	1	2
1983	17	8	7	1	0	1
1984	14	5	4	0	4	1
1985	6	3	3	0	0	0
1986	17	9	5	0	3	0
1987	16	5	9	0	0	2
1988	14	3	4	0	5	2
1989	19	6	7	0	4	2
1990	13	3	4	1	3	2
1991	13	3	7	1	2	0
1992	21	5	10	1	5	0
1993	12	3	8	0	1	0
1994	11	2	6	0	3	0
1995	14	3	3	0	8	0
1996	7	0	2	0	5	0
1997	5	1	1	1	2	0
1998	7	6	0	0	1	0
1999	2	1	0	0	1	0
2000	4	1	2	0	1	0
2001	5	0	2	1	1	1
2002	6	1	0	0	5	0
2003	8	2	2	0	4	0
2004	5	0	2	0	3	0
2005	2	1	0	0	1	0
2006	2	1	0	0	1	0
2007[5]	1	0	0	0	1	0

Source: Defence Statistics (Health)
Notes:
1.	Figures are for regular and reservist personnel.
2.	Excludes Road Traffic Accidents (RTA).
3.	As confirmed at a coroner's inquest.

BY THEIR VALOUR

4. From 14 August 1969.
5. Up to 31 July 2007.

Table 3: UK Armed Forces1 non hostile2 deaths as a result of Operation Banner by gender and cause, 14 August 1969 to 31 July 2007, numbers

Gender	All	Natural Causes	Accidents (exc RTA)	Assaults	Suicide or open verdicts[3]	Cause not known
All	483	144	209	12	73	45
Male	473	140	206	11	72	44
Female	10	4	3	1	1	1

Source: Defence Statistics (Health)
Notes:
1. Figures are for regular and reservist personnel.
2. Excludes Road Traffic Accidents (RTA).
3. As confirmed at a coroner's inquest.

For data prior to 1984, Defence Statistics have access to the Armed Forces Memorial (AFM) database owned by the tri-Service Joint Casualty and Compassionate Centre. The AFM database was created in order to identify Service personnel whose names were to be, and continue to be engraved on the Armed Forces Memorial at the National Arboretum in Staffordshire.

The AFM database records the deaths of all personnel who have died in Service since 1st Jan 1948, and for those who were killed or who died in Palestine from 1st Aug 1945 to 31st Aug 1948. Please note, the AFM database is not regarded as a validated source of historical fatality information, therefore, it cannot be guaranteed to be 100% complete or accurate due to it being populated manually from Service files.

The data presented is not limited to those personnel who died specifically in Northern Ireland. It also includes those personnel who may have been aeromedically evacuated to other countries and subsequently died from their injuries.

APPENDIX 3

UK Armed Forces deaths as a result of operations in NI, Aug 1969 to 31 July 2007

Service	All	Terrorist Action	Other
All	1,441	722	719
Naval Service	34	26	8
Royal Navy	8	5	3
Royal Marines	26	21	5
Army	1,381	692	689
Regular Army (exc. RIR)	814	477	337
Royal Irish Regiment	67	7	60
General Service	4	1	3
Home Service	63	6	57
Ulster Defence Regiment	481	197	284
Territorial Army (exc RIR)	17	9	8
Other non-regular Army	2	2	2
Royal Air Force	26	4	22

Notes: 1) Figures are for in-service personnel only
2) Figures may include deaths that occurred outside NI but as a result of Irish terrorism
3) Includes accidents, natural causes (see Appendices) (Source: Defence Statistics, Health)[37]

[37] FOI Smyth 02-01-2013-160507-018 correspondence dated: 29 December 2012

10 BIBLIOGRAPHY

Alison, Miranda. Women and Political Violence: Female Combatants in Ethno-National Conflict. London: Routledge

Bell, Vicki, In Pursuit of Civic Participation: The Early Experiences of the Northern Ireland Civic Forum, 2000-2002, Political Studies, vol 52

Brady, Evelyn et al. In the Footsteps of Anne. Belfast: Shanway

Clar na mBan 'A Women's Agenda for Peace: Conference Report'

Fairweather E.Only the Rivers Run Free, Northern Ireland: the Women's War. London: Pluto Press

Hennessy, Thomas. The Evolution of the Troubles 1970 -72. Dublin: Irish Academic Press

Hinds Bronagh 'Women working for peace in Northern Ireland' in Galligan Y, Ward E and Wilford R. Contesting Politics: women in Ireland North and South. London: Westview

Para 9 Cm 3232. Northern Ireland: Ground rules for Substantive All-Party Negotiations. London: HMSO 1996

United Nations Entity for Gender Equality and the Empowerment of Women. Report of the Fourth UN Conference on Women.Beijing, 1995
English, Richard. Armed Struggle: The History of the IRA. London: Pan

Eirigi, 'Imperialism – Ireland and Britain' 2007

Matthews, Ann. Dissidents: Irish Republican Women 1923-41. Dublin: Mercier

McEvoy, Sandra. Women Loyalist Paramilitaries in Northern Ireland: Duty, Agency and Empowerment - A Report from the Field". All Academic Research.

McGuffin, John. Internment. Dublin: Anvil

McKay, Susan. Northern Protestants: An Unsettled People. Dublin: Blackstaff

McMahon, Paul. British Spies and Irish Rebels: British Intelligence and Ireland, 1916-1945   . London: Boydell

McWilliams, Monica 'Struggling for Peace and Justice: Reflections on

Women's Activism in Northern Ireland' in 'Irish Women's Voice: Past and Present' Journal of Women's History 1995

Mowlam, Majorie. Momentum; The Struggle for Peace, Politics and the People. London: Hodder & Stoughton

Rawnsley, Andrew. Servants of the People: The Inside Story of New Labour. London: Penguin

Sales, Rosemary. Women Divided: Gender, religion and politics in Northern Ireland. London: Routledge

Ward, Margaret, Unmanageable Revolutionaries, Women and Irish Nationalism. London

Wood, Ian. Crimes of Loyalty: A History of the UDA. Edinburgh: University Press

ABOUT THE AUTHORS

Joanne McQuaid is a native of Derry City. She obtained her undergraduate degree in Modern History and Politics from Queen's University, Belfast in 2009. Her degree strongly embodied topics involving women's history and their role in politics, which created a long lasting love for the subject matter.

Emmet Doyle is a native of Derry and an Irish History and Politics graduate of Magee in the City. He is a former Junior Mayor of the City and a former Political Adviser in the Stormont Assembly.

NOTES

Printed in Poland
by Amazon Fulfillment
Poland Sp. z o.o., Wrocław